COME
TO THE
TABLE

John Mark Hicks

COME
TO THE
TABLE

REVISIONING
THE
LORD'S SUPPER

New
Leaf
Books

ORANGE, CALIFORNIA

COME TO THE TABLE
published by New Leaf Books

Copyright 2002 by John Mark Hicks

ISBN 0-9714289-7-2
Printed in the United States of America

Cover design by Kristi McTaggert, The ColorEdge, Costa Mesa, CA

For information:
New Leaf Books, 12542 S. Fairmont, Orange, CA 92869
1-877-634-6004 (toll free)

www.newleafbooks.org

02 03 04 05 06 07   9 8 7 6 5 4 3 2 1

Dedication

To the triune God who has acted at the Father's initiative through the Son's redemption in the fellowship of the Spirit so that his people might sit at table together, both in the present kingdom as well as in the one to come.

CONTENTS

Part IV: Communion Today: A Call for Supper Reform and Renewal

Conclusion

PREFACE

We are all shaped by our experience. When we think about "church," we conceive it in ways that approximate our experience. When we think about "preaching," we conceive it in accordance with our experience of preaching. When we think about the Lord's supper, our minds are filled with images from our experience. We think about pews in a church building, multiple-cup trays (perhaps even "one cup" for some), unleavened bread in the form of crackers, a man officiating from the pulpit, men standing behind a symbolic table with their arms formally crossed at the waist aligned in a meticulous order, silent meditation, and focused attention on the death of Christ.

But what was the practice of the Lord's supper like in the first century? Too easily we assume that our experience of the Lord's supper is equivalent to that of the primitive church. We lose a sense of historical perspective as we collapse our practice into theirs and assume their practice was functionally equivalent to ours. Actually, it appears that the practice of the supper in the early church was very different from ours. Their supper was home-based, a full meal with food and drink, an interactive fellowship at a table and characterized by joyous celebration.

The premise of this book is that our practice of the supper as a silent, solemn, individualistic eating of bread and drinking of wine is radically dissimilar from the joyous communal meal that united Christians in first century house churches. The contemporary practice of the supper needs to be "revisioned" according to biblical values. This is necessary because the contemporary form of the supper has reshaped its function. "Revisioning the Lord's supper" means understanding its original function for the purpose of reshaping the contemporary form to reflect the supper's theological values.

In a word, the supper should be revisioned as a "table" rather than an "altar." Altar is the dominant model for the supper in the contemporary church. It fosters individualism (privacy), silence, solemnity, and sorrow. To revision the supper as "table" will foster community, interactive communion, gratitude, and joy.

I will revision the supper as table by looking at biblical, historical, and theological materials. In conclusion, I offer specific, practical suggestions for reforming the practice of the supper in order to embody the vision of the supper as "table." I have written for the general audience because I think revisioning the table must be a bottom-up as well as a top-down concern. Only as the church as a community revisions the supper will the church renew the table dimensions of the supper. Consequently, I have often left to the side the technicalities of many points without, hopefully, sacrificing the argument itself.

This revisionist understanding of the supper has been forming in my mind for many years. I have taught this material in various settings and have learned much from the interaction. In particular, I am grateful for the students and faculty of both Harding University Graduate School of Religion and Lipscomb University with whom I have often discussed this material. Many churches have contributed to my understanding as they dialogued and even practiced some of the ideas in this book, including the Ross Road Church of Christ and Cordova Community Church in Memphis, TN, and the Woodmont Hills Church of Christ in Nashville, TN. I have presented it at various ministerial and congregational retreats in Japan, Korea, and

Germany as well as places in the United States (including the Minister's Seminar at the Institute for Christian Studies in Austin, TX). I have appreciated the opportunity to "test drive" these ideas, both in theory and practice.

I am also grateful for the invitation from Leonard Allen and New Leaf books to write this manuscript. It offers a wonderful opportunity to share my perspectives with a wider audience.

My recent experience of loss, through the death of my son on May 21, 2001 and my divorce on January 4, 2002, has deepened my appreciation for the experience of hope and reconciliation that the table embodies. My sense of family has been enhanced and my gratitude for my own family has deepened, particularly my brothers Mack and Jack (with his wife Carinda) Hicks, my sister Suzie McCarver, my nieces Allison and Brittney, my nephews Ian, Carson and Logan, my mother Lois Hicks, and my daughters Ashley and Rachel. The importance of the family table has come home to me and my hope is that that sense of table is adequately conveyed in this book. The church should be a place where family gathers at table together and experiences reconciliation, hope and joy.

My prayer is that this brief study will help churches rethink their understanding and practice of the Lord's supper. May God bless your reading and guide you into a fuller understanding of the gospel as it is shared with us at the table of the Lord.

John Mark Hicks
Nashville, Tennessee

1/ COMMUNION AS DIVINE INTENT

God never intended an altar, though he planned for it. Instead, God intended a table to enjoy the communion of his people. While the altar epitomizes the atoning work of God in forgiving sin, the table epitomizes the experience of communion.

The altar, the cross of Jesus Christ, was a means to an end. It was the penultimate act of God in order to bring about, through atonement, the ultimate intent of God, which is communion. The altar was an act of self-humiliation for the sake of the table. The altar, in terms of its goal, serves the table. The altar, by its atoning work, enables the table. Atonement secures communion. The cross grounds the table.

Communion as God's Creative Intent[1]

God's first gracious act toward humanity was not the Exodus nor the Cross, it was Creation. When God created, he acted freely and without compulsion. Humanity did not deserve to be created; it had no inherent right to exist. Neither was there some need which God had to satisfy through creation. God was not compelled by some inner necessity to create in order to preserve his own mental health. Creation was an act of unmerited love which arose freely out of God's will. God is praised in Revelation 4:11 because he created all things by his will. Creation was God's free decision and determined by his own will.

But why does God seek a communion of love with creatures? Is God a solitary figure who needs to create in order to have fellowship with others? Does God need company? The Christian doctrine of Trinity, which is the triune nature of God's life, answers these questions. In the light of God's revelation in Christ, we understand more about God's creative intent than is revealed in Genesis 1.

While the doctrine of "Trinity" (however that word may be defined, and it has variant meanings) seems remote, speculative and cumbersome to some, it is helpful in understanding God's purpose in creating the cosmos.[2] One does not have to be an astute theologian to recognize the impact that Trinitarian theology can have on understanding God's creative act. Indeed, Scripture reveals that creation was a Trinitarian act of God. God the Father is the fountainhead of creation; he is the source and origin of everything that exists. Everything in the universe originated with him; it was "from" him (Rom. 11:36; 1 Cor. 8:6). Yet, the Son is the instrument of creation. He is the means by which the Father created (John 1:1-3; 1 Cor. 8:6). The Father created nothing without the agency of the Son. The Spirit, as the breath of life, is God's dynamic presence which energizes life in the world (Job 26:13; 33:4; Psalm 33:6; 104:30). The Spirit was present at creation, and was the power by which life invaded what was lifeless (Gen. 1:2; 2:7). Creation, therefore, is from God the Father through the agency of the Son by the power of the Spirit. The one God, then, performed the mighty work of creation as a community just as that same God performs the mighty work of redemption as a triune community (cf. Eph. 2:18; 1 Pet. 1:2). Both creation and redemption are the work of the triune community.

The doctrine of the Trinity teaches that the divine reality is a community of loving fellowship between the Father, Son and

Spirit. It is a community of holy love. This communion of love explains why God created the cosmos. Even before the cosmos existed, there existed a community of love between the Father, Son and Spirit. Jesus prayed that his disciples might see the glory the Father had given him, and the Father gave him this glory because he loved him "before the foundation of the world" (John 17:24). This text provides a glimpse into the common life of the Father and Son before the act of creation. Before the cosmos existed, there existed a community of shared love (*agape*) between the Father and the Son.

The high priestly prayer of John 17 also points us to the redemptive love of God which flows from the love the Father has for the Son. Jesus promised his Father that he would continue to make the Father known to his disciples "so that the love with which you have loved me may be in them" (John 17:26). The intent of redemption is to bring the fallen world into the orbit of God's *agape* fellowship where just as the Father dwells in the Son and the Son in the Father, so God's people may dwell in them and they in God (John 17:21). God has acted in Christ Jesus in order that we might have fellowship with him. God's intent is that our fellowship might be with the Father and the Son (1 John 1:3). If the intent of redemption is modeled after creation, then the intent of creation is clear. God intended to create a people to share his loving community; to have fellowship with God through the sharing of his love. Creation is an expression of grace and love which engages his people in the fellowship of the Spirit (2 Cor. 13:14).

But this fellowship was not created by a solitary, lonely God. Before the creation of the world, God existed as a community, not as a solitary being. God did not create because he needed fellowship, since he already enjoyed fellowship through the triune communion of the Father, Son and Spirit. This fellowship was not created by God, as though at some point in time God became a fellowship. Rather, it is who God is. God is a community of love because God is *agape* (1 John 4:8). Consequently, God did not need to turn to anything outside of himself in order to experience loving fellowship and community. This was experienced in the mutual indwelling of God's Trinitarian fellowship.

The grace of God was expressed in the act of creation. The gracious act of creation, an act of agape love, is God's decision to share what he already possessed. It was not to gain something he lacked. Rather, God decided to share his own loving fellowship within the triune community with others. This is an astounding but wondrous thought. God, without compulsion, decided to share his holy communion with those whom he created. God created out of the overflow of his love. It flows from the inner-Trinitarian love which decided to share itself with others. God decided to express his love by creating us. Just as God so loved the world that he gave his Son, he also so loved that he created a world with which to share his love. God's love, by his free decision, is self-giving and other-centered so that it seeks to share the joy of the divine communion with others.

The best analogy for understanding this act of God—as limited as it is—is a couple's decision to have children. Why do couples decide to have children? Certainly, in a fallen world, there are less than pure motives. But in the purest sense, why do couples decide to have children? While there is a certain biological drive inherent in the human psyche, there is also the yearning to share our love. In the best of motives, couples decide to have children in order to share their love with another. When a couple decides to have a child, the couple has, in the best of circumstances, made a selfless decision. They have decided to share something that they could have kept to themselves. The love which exists between a husband and wife is a communion unsurpassed in human relations. When children are born into that loving communion, the children share something they did not create. The parents give something they were not compelled to share. Children, and we wish it were true in every instance, are born out of the loving communion between parents. They share their love with another.

When the Trinitarian community decided to create, they decided to share something they already enjoyed for the benefit of another. We humans did not create that fellowship, but it is offered to us in love. God created out of his love. He did not create in order to receive (as if he needed anything outside of himself), but he created to give and consequently experience the joy of communion with others. Thus, the act of creation is an act of grace, an act of selfless love.

Nevertheless, God does this for himself as well, just as parents gain value from having children and sharing the experience of love from another. God created for his own glory. Just as God created Israel for his own glory and marked off the church as his own possession to his own glory (Eph. 1:14), so God created the cosmos for his own glory (Isa. 43:7; 48:11). Creation was an act of God for God. Everything exists for him (Heb. 2:10; Rom. 11:36), that is, it for his glory, to his honor and for his benefit. God fills the whole earth with his glory (Num. 14:21) and displays his divine perfections throughout his creation (Psalm 8:1; 19:1). But this glory is ultimately found in fellowship with his creatures. It is not an egocentric glory. Creation is not an act of selfishness or self-aggrandizement. Rather, God glorifies himself in his fellowship with his people. This glory is not divorced from his holy love. His glory is expressed through his love. It is an other-centered love that gives and shares. The purpose of creation, therefore, is to magnify the glory of the God who shares his love and fellowship with those whom he has created.

God is glorified in the joy of communion with his creation. God delights in the communion of his people. Thus, God acts, whether in creation or redemption, to the praise of his glory which is expressed in the communion he has with his people (cf. Eph. 1:6,12,14). So also human beings exist to magnify and reflect the glory of God by enjoying fellowship with him.[3] God created in order to share his divine fellowship with others, and this is the foundational act of God's grace. This intent motivates the drama of redemption itself.

Communion as God's Redemptive Intent

The model for understanding God's gracious act of creation is God's two great redemptive acts (one of which prefigures the other): the creation of Israel and the creation of the church. Both of these moments in redemptive history reflect God's original intent as he sought to redeem his fallen creation. Consequently, the creation of Israel and the creation of church are the extension of God's original act of creation. God now seeks to redeem what has fallen; he seeks to re-create what has been destroyed. God's re-creation is driven by the same motive and interest that moved God to create in the first place. God decided to create, just as he decided to redeem, out of his love.

Israel did not create herself nor did she have some inherent, irresistible value as a nation. God was not compelled to call Abraham, nor was he obligated to choose Jacob over Esau (cf. Rom. 9:10-13). God did not choose Israel because they were so numerous—as if God must choose the largest nation, nor did he choose Israel because they were so faithful—as if any nation's righteousness could put God in their debt. Instead, God chose Abraham and Israel because he loved them. God chose Israel despite the fact that they were the "fewest of all peoples" and a "stubborn people" (Deut. 7:7; 9:6). God chose them because he loved them, and consequently sought to enter into covenant with them (Deut. 7:8-9).

As God created Israel to experience and delight in the communion of his people, so the table was at the center of this communion in Israel. The sacrificial meals in Israel were a communion with God, as chapters two and three will discuss. God invites Israel to share life with him at a table. Consequently, festive meals are the continuous experience of Israel's faith. The sacrificial altar brings the communion of a sacrificial meal. The atoning blood ritual of the altar enables the experience of communion at the table.

The church did not create herself nor did she have some inherent, irresistible value as a people. God was not compelled to send his Son, nor was he obligated to redeem fallen people from their sins. God did not elect us in Christ because we were so holy—as if we could pretend to be so holy, nor did he elect us in Christ because we are so inherently valuable—as if we could arrogantly claim that something is so wonderful about us that God had to redeem us. Rather, God chose us out of his loving grace which he gave us in Christ Jesus (Eph. 1:4-6). Christ died for us despite the fact that we were sinners and God's enemies (Rom. 5:6-10). God demonstrated his love for us through the gracious gift of his Son whom he put forth as an atonement for our sins. "God's love was revealed among us in this way" (1 John 4:9). This is God's redeeming love, and this same love moved God to create the cosmos in the first place. God created, just like he re-created, in order that he might share his love among us.

As God created the church to experience and delight in the communion of his people, so the table is at the center of this communion. The Lord's supper, the table, is a communion experience between God and his people, as chapters four through eight will discuss. God invites the church to share his life at a table. Thus, at the center of the life and worship of the early church was the "breaking of bread." The sacrificial altar brings the communion of the sacrificial meal. The atoning blood ritual of the cross enables the experience of communion at the table.

God intended community in creation and thus community in redemption. And he intended this community to commune

with him. God created a community—a male and a female who
would fill the earth with their descendants, and consequently
fill the earth with God's glory (Gen. 1:28; 9:1). When God created Israel, he chose Abraham and Sarah whose descendants
would be a people, a nation which would be the light of God's
glory among the other nations. When God created the church,
he chose Christ who would be the author of salvation for the
brothers and sisters he would bring to glory (Heb. 2:10). God
has always intended a people for himself. Whether in the original act of creation or in the redemptive act of re-creation, God
gathers a people for himself.

This is a pervasive theme in Scripture. When God entered
into a covenant of circumcision with Abraham, he promised
him that he would not only be Abraham's God, but the God of
his descendants after him. The promise meant that Abraham's
descendants would be God's people and he would be their
God (Gen. 17:7-8). When God came to Israel in Egypt through
Moses, he promised them redemption and assured them that "I
will take you as my people, and I will be your God" (Ex. 6:7).
When Israel set up the tabernacle in the wilderness, God's
glory descended upon it with the promise that there God
would dwell among his people and be their God (Ex. 29:45;
40:34-35; Lev. 26:11-12). The indwelling of God's presence was
repeated with the completion of the temple under Solomon (1
Kings 8:11; 2 Chron. 5:14; 7:1-3). The prophets constantly
reminded the people of God's promise to be present among
them (Ezek. 34:30). Israel would be God's people and he
would be their God (Jer. 7:23; 11:4; 24:7; Ezek. 11:20; 14:11;
36:28; 37:27; Zech. 2:11; 8:8; 13:9).

Further, this promise was at the heart of the "new
covenant." Jeremiah announced God's promise of a new
covenant in response to Israel's unfaithfulness to the old.
Through Jeremiah, God declared his intent to forgive Israel's sin
so that he could fulfill his promise among them, that is, the

promise that "I will be their God, and they shall be my people" (Jer. 31:33). Paul, in the context of thinking about the ministry of this new covenant (2 Cor. 3:6), reminds us that this promise has found expression in God's church where "we are the temple of the living God" (2 Cor. 6:16). The church as the temple of God means that Leviticus 26:11-12 has been fulfilled in the church, as God has said: "I will live in them and walk among them, and I will be their God, and they shall be my people" (2 Corinthians 6:16 quoting Leviticus). In the church God has a people for himself.

This redemptive-historical motif, that God seeks a people for himself, demonstrates that God's intent in redemption/ re-creation is to dwell with his people in a communion of love. God seeks fellowship with his people. He created a community, a people, for himself. God wanted to share community with his creation in loving fellowship. He created for the sake of a table, and he recreates to experience that table once again.

Communion as God's Eschatological Goal

While Israel and the church were divine creations for the sake of communion, the ultimate goal of the covenantal promise is the eschatological dwelling of God with his people in a community which he will establish when the new age is consummated. When the new Jerusalem descends out of heaven, then a loud voice will announce: "See the home of God is among mortals. He will dwell with them as their God; they will be his peoples, and God himself will be with them" (Rev. 21:3). The communion that God intended in creation he will recreate in the eschaton, that is, in the new heaven and new earth. There, too, God will invite his people to share his life at a table.

Isaiah 25:6-9 anticipates a day when God will wipe away every tear through swallowing up the disgrace of his people. That disgrace is the burial shroud which covers all people, that is, death. On the day when God destroys death, he will celebrate with his people in an eschatological banquet with rich (fatty) food and the best (aged) wine. When God has conquered all his enemies, including death, he will throw a celebration banquet with his people as honored guests.

God will sponsor a banquet on Mount Zion in Jerusalem and he will take away death. God will replace the mourning and tears of death with the rejoicing of life and salvation. God will turn mourning into dancing. God will save his people who trust in him by destroying death and hosting a festive celebration at a table in his holy presence. God promises to live among his people where death is destroyed and there are no more tears.

The New Testament applies the language of Isaiah 25 to the consummation. Paul quotes this text as he celebrates the victory of life over death in the resurrection (1 Cor. 15:54). Rev. 7:17 and 21:4 place God's removal of tears from the eyes of his people in the eschaton. The Old Testament expected a time when the earth would be consumed and judged (Isaiah 24), but also a time when death itself would be destroyed. Isaiah 25 expects the consummation—the destruction of death. It expects a new heaven and new earth (Isa. 65:17-19). It expects a heavenly banquet in God's presence. This is the essence of the eschaton. God's goal in redemption is to destroy death and renew communion with his people, a communion he intended in creation. God's goal is a table.

In the New Testament this eschatological banquet is a Messianic one. God will spread the messianic banquet for his people in the new heaven and new earth. All of his people from all nations will sit down with each other to enjoy fellowship with their God and with each other (cf. Matt. 8:10-12; Luke 13:29). It will be a covenant meal in which God will fully dwell with his people (Rev. 21:3). The new Jerusalem will have a river of water which waters the tree of life that bears "kinds of fruit" for the nations (Rev. 22:1-2). God will commune with his people at a table forever.

Conclusion

The story of creation reveals God's intent. He intended communion and life. God created life, provided sustenance, and offered the tree of life as a table of life from which the people of God might eat. God created a community to image and represent the harmony, joy, and fellowship of his own triune community. He shared his dominion with those who bore his image so that they could serve as his representatives upon the earth. He intended his people to fill the earth with their children so that he might delight in their love through communion with them.

God's story in Scripture highlights this intent. From beginning to end, from creation to eschaton, God desires a people for himself with whom he can share a loving fellowship. God desires, to put it in New Testament language, *koinonia* (fellowship, communion). In redemption God has called us into the "fellowship of his Son" (1 Cor. 1:9) to enjoy the "communion (*koinonia*) of the Holy Spirit" (2 Cor. 13:13) as we also experience the "fellowship" of the Father (1 John 1:3). In redemption God offers us his triune fellowship just as he did in creation. Christians have all been baptized into the fellowship of the Father, Son and Holy Spirit (Matt. 28:19). In both creation and redemption, this fellowship is God's goal, and it guides all his actions in the world. It is the fundamental structural principle of God's story. God intends to commune with a people he calls his own.

At the center of that intent is the experience of communion at table. The altar, with its blood ritual, is God's act of atonement for the sake of reconciliation. God forgives through the cross. But the goal of atonement is *koinonia* (fellowship). The goal of the cross is the table. The cross restores the communion that God created in the beginning; the altar enables the table. Just as God always intended communion, so he always intended a table. The table is the experience of communion.

Questions for Discussion

1. Why did God create the cosmos? How does God's nature as a triune community and his loving nature shape our understanding of God's creation of community?

2. How does "table" reflect God's desire for fellowship, communion and community? How does this table appear in various stages of God's history with his people (Israel, church and in the new heaven and new earth)?

3. Which is God's goal—the table or the altar? What is the relationship between the table and the altar?

4. How does this central theme of communion in Scripture affect your understanding of the Lord's supper?

PART I.

COMMUNION IN ISRAEL: EATING WITH GOD

2 / COVENANT MEALS

Since creation God has sought covenant relationship with his creatures in order to establish community. After the fall, God entered into covenant with Abraham and his descendants, and ultimately with all the nations, toward the eschatological end of eternal communion. God's covenant desire is to be our God and we to be his people. Throughout the history of God's redemptive work, God has established fellowship and covenant through sacrifice (Ps. 50:5) and has confirmed that fellowship and covenant through eating the sacrifice, a meal. Those meals within redemptive history anticipate the eschatological messianic banquet when God will dwell with his people in the new Jerusalem. The "Lord's supper" is the present stage of this redemptive-historical trajectory of covenant meals. Since it embraces the past and anticipates the future, the full meaning of this Christian meal can only be understood in the light of redemptive history.

The most inclusive disclosure of this meaning might be the category of "covenant meal." The idea of "covenant" embodies relationship. A covenant between two persons is a relational bond rooted in the gracious initiative of one toward the other.

It is a gracious commitment that engenders reciprocity and mutuality. A "covenant meal" seals and celebrates this commitment. By sacrifice the two parties make a covenant (literally in Hebrew "cut a covenant") as they bind themselves together in mutual commitment and celebrate their new relationship by eating the sacrifice in a covenant meal. The altar establishes the covenant and the table celebrates it. The altar produces reconciliation and the table is the experience of that reconciliation. By sacrifice God makes a covenant with Israel and then invites them to sit at table in covenantal communion.

A Covenant Meal

The Hebrew Bible refers to "making a covenant" as "cutting a covenant" because covenantal rituals involved animal sacrifices. The animals were laid on the ground in halves opposite each other so that the covenanters could walk between them. As the parties to the covenant walked down the aisle between the animals they invoked a self-imprecatory oath: "May what was done to this animal be done to me if I do not keep this covenant." If they failed to keep the covenant, then death was the sentence. Jeremiah 34:18 reflects this understanding when God speaks through the prophet: "And those who transgressed my covenant and did not keep the terms of the covenant that they made before me, I will make like the calf when they cut it in two and passed between its parts." The covenantal commitment was serious and walking between the pieces placed one under a curse.

God himself participates in these covenants. Just as worshippers slaughter the animals and walk between them, so God also walks between them. The most vivid example of this is Genesis 15 when God covenants with Abraham. God promises Abraham that his heir will come from his own body, his descendants will be like the stars of the sky, and they will possess the land of Canaan (Gen. 15:4-5, 7, 18-19). That day God "cut a covenant" with Abraham (Gen. 15:18). As a participant in the covenant, God passed between the halves of the animals (cf. Gen. 15:10). "When the sun had gone down and it was dark," Genesis 15:17 reads, "a smoking fire pot and a flaming torch passed between these pieces." The fire was the presence of God who secures his commitment to the covenant by passing between the halves of the animals.

The slaughtered animals, however, were not left on the ground to rot or be eaten by birds. They were eaten as part of the covenantal meal which celebrated the covenant. The altar and the concomitant "passing" ritual were followed by a table of joy and celebration.

Genesis 31:22-55 provides an example of a covenant meal within a family clan. After working for Laban for twenty years and sensing the growing hostility between Laban's family and himself (Gen. 31:1-2), at the Lord's prompting, Jacob decided to return to his ancestral land (Gen. 31:3). Jacob and his family slipped away. Laban pursued with hostile intent and caught up with Jacob in Gilead (Gen. 31:22-23). But God intervened and told Laban not to harm Jacob (Gen. 31:24).

As a result, Laban offered to make a covenant with Jacob (Gen. 31:44): "let us make a covenant, you and I, and let it be a witness between you and me." The covenant would be a witness between Jacob and Laban of their peaceful relationship. God would not only be a witness to the covenant, but a participant in blessing the parties involved as well as a judge between them (Gen. 31:49-50, 53). Both Laban and Jacob swore an oath, and a sacrifice was offered to enact the covenant which was followed by a meal to celebrate and confirm it (Gen. 31:54). The meal was a symbol of peace and mutual acceptance within the clan. It celebrated and sealed the peace which now existed between Laban and Jacob.

Another example of a covenant meal is found in Genesis 26:28-31. Abimelech, the king of the Philistines, came to Isaac in order to "cut a covenant" between them. The mutual agreement meant that neither would do either any harm and that peace would exist between them under the blessing of the Lord. As a symbol of friendship and peace, Isaac "made them a feast, and they ate and drank" (Gen. 26:30). Apparently, Isaac sacrificed animals on the altar he had just built at Beersheba in response to God's renewal of the Abrahamic promise (Gen. 26:23-25). God renewed his covenant with Isaac and Isaac entered into covenant with Abimelech—both covenants involved altar and table. The altar "cut the covenant" and the table celebrated it.

God Covenants with Israel (Exodus 24)

The Exodus was an act of God's grace by which he redeemed Israel from Egyptian bondage. Exodus 15 declares this redemptive act in song, and it is on this ground that Israel is invited into covenant with God. At the Red Sea, God redeemed Israel. But the Exodus was not God's goal; it was his means. God's goal is to dwell among his people and enter into covenant with them. The Exodus was a necessary means toward that end. God redeems into order to take Israel as his own people so they will know (share intimacy) that the Lord is their God (Ex. 6:7). God redeems in order to covenant. He redeems in order to enjoy communion with his people through the gift of his presence.

Exodus 19-24 tells the story of Israel's covenanting with God. God announces his intention to establish a covenantal relationship with Israel, and the people accept (Ex. 19:3-8). The covenant is summarized in the Decalogue (Ex. 20:1-17) and then explained more fully in the "book of the covenant" (Ex. 21-23). Finally, the covenant is ratified through bloody sacrifices and a meal (Ex. 24).

God brought Israel to his holy mountain at Sinai in Exodus 19. God encountered his people at this mountain and gave his holy presence to them. God declared his intent to come to his people in a "dense cloud" (Ex. 19:9) and settle on the holy mountain. There Moses led the people out to "meet God" as they stood at the foot of the mountain (Ex. 19:17). The mountain was covered with "a thick cloud," which emitted "thunder and lightning" (Ex. 19:16). The mountain rumbled and shook with the presence of the holy God. The mountain was holy because the holy God had come down to dwell on it in the presence of his people. Consequently, the people were warned not to touch the mountain and the priests were admonished to consecrate themselves (Ex. 19:22). Indeed, all Israel was to prepare to meet God (Ex. 19:10). The penalty for violating God's holiness was death (Ex. 19:12-13).

When God invited Israel to enter into covenant with him in Exodus 19:4-6, the people responded with a resounding "yes" (Ex. 19:7-8). They committed to be the holy nation which the covenant demanded. They would be a kingdom of consecrated priests. Exodus 20-23 explains the meaning of this holiness. The Decalogue (Ex. 20:1-17) provides ethical boundaries for God's people. The Book of the Covenant (Ex. 21-23) provides case laws to guide the application of the Decalogue to the specific situations which Israel will face in their journey to the land of promise. The fundamental principle of covenantal expectation is that the people will be holy, just as God is holy. God calls them to live out these ethical principles because "You shall be people consecrated to me" (Ex. 22:31). The holiness of God elicits a response of holiness from his people.

At the same time, God provides the means by which his people may commune with him. He provides a table. The Book of the Covenant prescribes three celebrative festivals where "all your males are to appear before the Lord God" (Ex. 23:17). The three festivals (Ex. 23:15-16) are Passover ("unleavened bread"), Pentecost ("harvest"), and Tabernacles ("ingathering"). Israel meets God at the festivals as they each involve sacrificial meals.

God calls Israel to meet him at a table and enjoy his holy communion. Indeed, Israel is called to make an "altar" and "sacrifice on it your burnt offerings and your offerings of well-being" where God "will come" to them and "bless" them (Ex. 20:24). God meets his people at a table.

In Exodus 24:1-11, Israel enters into covenant with God, which is ratified through burnt offerings and fellowship offerings (Ex. 24:5). The structure reveals the text's emphasis.

> A. God invites Moses and the elders into his presence (24:1-2).
> > B. The word of the Lord is spoken and the people affirm the covenant (24:3).
> > > C. The words are written by Moses (24:4a).
> > > > D. The sacrifices are offered (24:4b-6).
> > > C. The words are read by Moses (24:7a).
> > B. The people affirm the covenant and the blood is sprinkled (24:7b-8).
> A. Moses and the elders eat and drink in the presence of God (24:9-11).

The description begins and ends with divine presence. God invites Moses and the elders to come up on the mountain and they go up (Ex. 24:1-2, 9-11). The people affirm their willingness to keep the covenant (Ex. 24:3, 7b-8), and the "book of the covenant" is written and read by Moses (Ex. 24:4a, 7a). In the center are the sacrificial offerings (Ex. 24:4b-6). At the heart of this pericope are altar and table. The altar (sacrifices) is the ground upon which Moses and the elders are invited into the presence of God to eat and drink at a table.

Moses sprinkled the "blood of the covenant" on the people (Ex. 24:7-8). Through blood, God establishes covenant with his people (cf. Heb. 9:20-22). It is in the wake of this event that the leaders of Israel went up and "saw the God of Israel" (Ex.

24:10). God neither rejects nor consumes them with his holiness, but rather accepts them into his presence on the ground of his gracious covenant of blood. On the mountain, the leaders of Israel eat and drink in the presence of God. Exodus 24:11 states: "they beheld God, and they ate and drank."

The significance of this statement is immense. The God of Israel is a Holy God who cannot be approached by sinful human beings (cf. Ex. 33:20). No one could touch the holy mountain because of God's presence. But God establishes communion with his people through covenantal sacrifice. This communion is expressed in the statement that they "saw God," which is stated twice for emphasis. It is an astounding statement—Moses and the elders "saw God." They experienced his holy presence without being consumed by his holiness. They had been made holy by the blood of the sacrifices and now they enter God's presence. But more than that, they also experienced communion with God through a covenantal meal. They shared fellowship with God at a table. God becomes the God of his people through covenant, and this covenant is celebrated through a meal.

The text depicts the relationship between altar and table. The altar is the blood ritual. It is the moment of atonement and forgiveness. God cleanses his people with blood. But the altar is followed by a table. At the table, Moses and the elders "saw God" and ate in his presence. The blood of the covenant establishes our relationship with God so that we may eat in his presence as we affirm our allegiance to the covenant, participate in the forgiveness of the altar and experience the presence of God at the table. The table is the experience of reconciliation and fellowship. While the altar may be a time of sadness, penance and guiltiness, the table is a time of joy, communion and commitment.

The Lord's supper recalls this event. In Matthew 26:27, Jesus describes the fruit of the vine as his "blood of the covenant," an allusion to Exodus 24:8. The blood is the enactment of the covenant. The shedding of blood in Exodus 24 is paralleled with the cross in Hebrews 9:15-22. The cross is the Christian altar and the Lord's supper is the Christian table. Just as the cross brings forgiveness and reconciliation, so the Lord's supper is the experience of communion in God's presence.

Covenant Renewal in Israel

In Israel, "eating and drinking" within a sacrificial context is eating and drinking "in the presence of God." God is present among his people as witness, judge and participant. This is stressed in many contexts. For example, Jethro brought Moses and the elders of Israel the sacrificial meat he had offered to God and he ate with them "in the presence of God" (Ex. 18:12). The Passover is a family meal where families "eat" in the "presence of the Lord your God, you and your households, rejoicing in all the undertakings in which the Lord your God has blessed you." (Deut. 12:7). Sacrifices should be eaten "in the presence of the Lord your God" (Deut. 12:18; cf. 14:23, 26; 15:20). When Israel eats its sacrifices, it eats in the presence of God.

The most significant expressions of the covenantal dimension of these sacrificial meals are the many "covenant renewal" events in the history of Israel. These events are times when Israel gathered to rededicate themselves to the covenant and in the presence of God pledge their allegiance to him. The table symbolized their commitment and dedication to the covenant as they communed with God through eating and drinking.

One important covenant renewal occurred when Israel entered the promised land (Josh. 8:30-35). Deuteronomy 27:1-8 contains the instructions that Israel followed as they approached Mount Ebal. There Israel built an altar and sacrificed burnt offerings and fellowship offerings. Significantly, Israel is commanded to "make sacrifices of well-being, and eat them there, rejoicing before the Lord your God" (Deut. 27:7).

Again, the distinction between altar and table emerges. The altar is where the animals are sacrificed, but the table is where the animals are eaten. The altar is a blood ritual, but the table is the experience of divine presence characterized by celebration and joy.

Another occasion of renewal and recommitment is the building of the temple in 2 Chronicles 5-7. As the ark was carried into the temple, "so many sheep and oxen" were sacrificed "that they could not be numbered or counted" (2 Chron. 5:6). These were sacrificed "before the Lord," including 22,000 oxen and 120,000 sheep (2 Chron. 7:4-5). These sacrifices included "fellowship offerings" (NIV) or "offerings of well-being" (2 Chron. 7:7), which meant that the people ate the meat of the sacrifice in a covenant meal. The people celebrated the completion of the temple for fourteen days and returned home "joyful and in good spirits because of the goodness that the Lord had shown to David and to Solomon and to his people Israel" (2 Chron. 7:10).

Another occasion of covenant renewal is the rebuilding of the temple at the time of return from Babylonian captivity (Ezra 6:13-22). The people dedicated the newly rebuilt temple with the sacrifice of hundreds of animals (Ezra 6:17) and then celebrated the Passover in the appropriate month (Ezra 6:19). These events were characterized by "joy" as Israel celebrated God's goodness and his sovereign purpose to complete his temple (Ezra 6:16, 22).

Another occasion of covenant renewal is the rebuilding of the walls of Jerusalem (Neh. 7:73b-8:18). Israel gathered to celebrate the Feast of Trumpets (Num. 29:1-6) in order to renew their covenant with God and remember his blessings. Ezra read the law to the assembly on the first day of the Feast and led the people in worship. This day was explicitly a day of joy and the people were forbidden to "mourn or weep" (Neh. 8:9). Instead, they were to "enjoy choice food and sweet drinks" as part of the festive celebration (Neh. 8:10, NIV). The people responded by eating and drinking as they celebrated with "great rejoicing" for seven days (Neh. 8:12, 18). In addition, the people shared with those who had "nothing prepared" (Neh. 8:10, NIV). Festivals were occasions to share food with the poor and needy (cf. Esther 9:19, 22). As the people of God remember their own blessings, they are called to share God's gifts with others (cf. Psalm 112). Thus, the eating and drinking of festive celebrations was inclusive, even including aliens in the land (cf. 2 Chron. 30:25).

Conclusion

Several themes coalesce in the covenant meal. First, there is a distinction between the altar and the table. The altar is the blood ritual, which may be characterized by sadness, guilt and penance. But the table is a different moment with a different mood. The table is shaped by joy and communion. It is a festive celebration. There is always joy at the table. They are not sad occasions.

Second, Israel eats in the presence of God. God is not absent, but is present through communion and fellowship. Israel eats with God in these meals. God is a participant because he is a party to the covenant. God's presence is his commitment to the covenant. He will faithfully fulfill his promises. It is a moment where God shares his holy presence with his people and renews his own commitment to his people.

Third, as Israel eats there is a sense of renewal and commitment. Israel remembers God's works on their behalf. They celebrate God's goodness and faithfulness. In response, Israel eats with renewed commitment to the covenant. It is a time of rededication.

The Lord's supper reflects these same themes. The supper is a table, not an altar. The church eats in the presence of God as Jesus, the living host, eats with us at the table. The church comes to the table with commitment and a sense of renewal. When the church eats and drinks at the table of the Lord, it eats and drinks a covenant meal. Just as Israel ate, so the church continues to eat—in the presence of God, with covenantal commitment and at a table.

Questions for Discussion

1. What is a "covenant meal"? How does the idea of "covenant" function in the Lord's supper?

2. If no one can "see" God, what is meant and how is it possible that Moses, Aaron and the elders of Israel "saw" God on Mount Sinai? In what sense did they "see" God?

3. What is a "covenant renewal" event? How is the Lord's supper a "covenant renewal"? How is such a renewal a two-way street between God and humanity?

4. What is the mood of a "covenant renewal" meal? Solemn? Serious? Joyous?

3 / SACRIFICES AS FELLOWSHIP MEALS

Most Christians are unfamiliar with the sacrifices of the Hebrew Bible. There are many reasons for this. They range from a neglect of the Old Testament in general to a neglect of Leviticus in particular as well as our cultural unfamiliarity with sacrifices. We have never experienced a sacrificial ritual. Moreover, most have never seen an animal slaughtered much less the blood rituals of Old Testament sacrifices. Unfortunately, this not only means a lack of appreciation for Israel's religion, but also a lack of understanding regarding the Lord's supper.

When the apostle Paul wanted to explain the meaning of the Lord's supper to Corinth, he pointed them to the sacrifices of Israel. If they would reflect on the meaning of Israel's sacrifices, then they could appreciate the meaning of the Lord's supper. "Consider the people of Israel," Paul wrote, "are not those who eat the sacrifices partners in the altar?" (1 Cor. 10:18). Eat the sacrifices? Most people do not realize that the sacrificial ritual included a meal where the participants ate the sacrificial meat as a fellowship meal. That picture, however, is what Paul evokes in the minds of the Corinthians to facilitate their understanding of the significance of the Lord's supper.

Instead of appealing specifically to the Passover as the back-ground for understanding the Lord's supper, Paul alludes to the whole sacrificial system. The Passover is one of the sacrifices of Israel, but it is not the only one. Paul calls us to consider the meaning of Israel's sacrificial meals in order to understand the Lord's supper. To understand one is to understand the other.

The Sacrifices of Israel

Sacrifices were gifts offered to God which functioned to remove sin and sanctify a place/person for the presence of God. The goal of sacrifices were to make a holy space in which God could dwell. Thus, the blood of sacrifices were sprinkled on furniture, books and locales. It sanctified them. It created holy space. In the same way, sacrifices sanctified people so that God could dwell among them. The goal of a sacrifice, then, was the experience of divine presence and communion. They are the means by which the worshipper drew near to God and entered into communion with God's holy presence.

The three major festive sacrifices are: sin offering, burnt offering and fellowship offering. Leviticus 9 provides the para-digmatic meaning of these sacrifices as they are offered when the Aaronic priesthood is inaugurated. The sin offering is the atonement offering; it expiates or removes sin (Lev. 9:8-11). The burnt offering represents the consecration or dedication of the worshipper to God; it is wholly burned up to God as the whole animal is given to him (Leviticus 9:12-14). The fellow-ship offering is an expression of the peace/fellowship or rec-onciliation that exists between God and the worshipper (9:18-21). In consequence of the three sacrifices, the glory of the Lord appeared to the people (9:22-24).

Whereas the burnt offering is wholly burned up to God (the Greek translation of the Hebrew word is holocaust), the sin and fellowship offerings are eaten in a sacrificial meal while the fat is burned on the altar to God. The sin offering is eaten by the priests, but the fellowship offering is eaten by both priests and worshippers. The fellowship offering is the only sacrifice which the worshippers eat (the Passover is a form of fellowship offering; cf. Deut. 16:1-4). Paul alludes to this sacrifice when contemplating the meaning of the Lord's supper.

Leviticus 3:1-17; 4:10,26,31,35; and 7:11-38 describe the various types of "fellowship" (NIV) or "well-being" (NRSV) offerings. This term is variously translated "fellowship," "welfare," "communion," "shared-offering," "peace," or "well-being" (from the Hebrew term *shelem*, which many believe is related to the normal Hebrew term for "peace" [*shalom*]). The sacrifice establishes fellowship through its expiatory significance (compare Lev. 3:1-5 with 17:11), but it primarily exhibits fellowship (peace) between God and the worshipper through a covenant meal. Eichrodt describes the significance of the sacrifice in this way: "At such a festival [covenant renewal] the common meal denotes physical entry into a new association, a fact that emerges with especial emphasis from the account of the feast of the seventy elders on Sinai in the presence of the covenant God."[1]

Of the major sacrifices, this is the only offering where the worshipper eats part of the sacrifice. The sacrificial offering becomes a meal in which bread and drink are also present (cf. Lev. 7:12-15; Ps. 116:13-17). The meal celebrates the relationship between the participants in the meal, and everyone shares in this meal—the Lord (Lev. 3:3-4), the priest (Lev. 7:28), and the worshipper. God, the priest and the worshipper share *shalom* through the meal. It exhibits the harmony, peace and well-being of that relationship. The theological significance of the meal is that it displays in a concrete way the peace that exists between God, the worshipper and the community. Again, Eichrodt summarizes the point well in this extended note:

The special character which the communion with the deity mediated in this way acquired in Israel can only be rightly defined by reference to the nation's unique conception of God. This sacred meal is certainly concerned with the real presence of the deity and that personal union with him from which all life and strength derive...The power of the sacral communion mediated by the sacrifice rests rather on God's declaration that he is prepared to enter into a special relationship with his people and to give them a share in his own life. The communion sacrifice becomes a sacrament, in which the blessing pronounced by the priest, the hymn sung to the glory of God, the casting of oracles and the promulgation of law carried out in conjunction with the ritual, all recall men to the exalted power of their divine Lord and Judge, whose fellowship they are experiencing in the celebration.[2]

The Fellowship Offering

Since understanding the sacrificial ritual and meal is significant for understanding the Lord's supper, it is important to give some attention to what this ritual involved, especially since modern Christians are so unfamiliar with the ritual. The following description is essentially what a first century Jew would have witnessed at the Jerusalem temple.[3]

The day before the ritual the worshippers immersed themselves before nightfall. As they entered the temple, they may have immersed themselves again in one of the baths provided at the foot of the Temple Mount. The worshippers brought an animal from the herd or flock with them. The worshippers laid their hands on the animal to declare the intention of the sacrifice. The sacrifice could be dedicated to thanksgiving as gratitude for any blessing in the life of the worshipper (Lev. 7:12). The sacrifice could also be dedicated to a vow before the Lord, or even a "freewill" expression of happiness (Lev. 7:16). The sacrifice also included a bread offering with yeast (Lev. 7:12-13; thus, leavened bread instead of unleavened bread), as well as a drink offering (cf. Ps. 116:13-17). The sacrifice, therefore, was a meal with meat, bread and drink (cf. Num. 6:17; 15:1-12).

The worshipper killed the animal. Usually, this would be performed by slitting the throat. The priest standing with the worshipper would catch the blood in a bowl and pour it around the temple altar. The animal was then taken to a place in the temple to be butchered by a Levite. When the meat was returned, the fat was burned on the altar to God as "a food offering" since "all the fat is the Lord's" (Lev. 3:11, 16-17). The worshipper took the breast and waved it before the Lord as a gift to God. The worshipper, then, gave the breast and right thigh to the priest. The priest took his portion home to share with his family (Lev. 7:14). The worshipper took the rest to his home for a festive meal with family and friends. Since the thank offering had to be eaten the same day (Lev. 7:12) and the votive offering had to be eaten within two days (Lev. 7:16), the meal was intended to be shared with others. It was not an individualistic act. On the contrary, the law designed it as a communal act since one could not eat a young bull (on average 800 pounds of meat) alone on the same day.

The communal dimension of the meal is extremely significant. The meal involves God, priest and the worshippers (including their family and friends, or even their larger community). The community participates in the meal. God is a participant as well. The meal exhibits the relational dimensions of Israel's faith. No one eats alone. No one eats in isolation. Israel eats as a community in fellowship with God and each other. It is a familial act where worshippers sit at table with family and friends in the presence of God.

The Fellowship Meal in the Hebrew Bible

The fellowship meal appears regularly in the pages of the Hebrew Bible. It is shared at the ratification of the Mosaic covenant (Ex. 20:24; 24:5). It inaugurates the priesthood (Lev. 9:4, 18, 22). It is part of every major festival, including Passover, Pentecost and Tabernacles (cf. Num. 29:39). It is the sacrifice eaten at the conclusion of the Nazirite vow (Num. 6:13-17). It was part of the covenant renewal at Shechem on Mount Ebal (Deut. 27:7; Josh. 8:31). It was eaten at the inauguration of Saul (1 Sam. 11:15). Israel celebrated the arrival of the ark of the covenant into Jerusalem by eating fellowship offerings (2 Sam. 6:17; 1 Chron. 16:1-2). David offered a fellowship offering in order to end the plague that enveloped Jerusalem (2 Sam. 24:25). It was eaten at the inauguration of Solomon (1 Chron. 29:21-22). Solomon offered it as a thanksgiving in response to God's promises of blessings in his life (1 Kings 3:15). Fellowship offerings were eaten at the dedication of the temple (1 Kings 9:25; 2 Chron. 7:7).

Fellowship meals were also part of Hezekiah's two-week Passover celebration (2 Chron. 29:35; 30:22), and they were part of the normal temple celebrations (2 Chron. 31:2). When Manasseh was restored to the throne by God's grace, he offered fellowship offerings in celebration (2 Chron. 33:16). Ezekiel describes the frequent use of fellowship offerings in the rebuilt temple he envisions (Ezek. 43:27; 45:15, 17; 46:2, 12). Indeed, the fellowship sacrifice would have been a daily occurrence as various people brought thanksgiving offerings to the temple.

In addition, the thanksgiving offering is prominent in the Psalms. Worshippers would bring an offering to give thanks for something God had done in their lives. For example, Psalm 116 is a thanksgiving Psalm. The worshipper had prayed for heal-ing during a time of impending death. God heard his cry and healed him. In gratitude, the Psalmist asks (116:12): "What shall I return to the Lord for all his bounty to me?" He responds to his own question (116:13-14): "I will lift up the cup of salvation and call on the name of the Lord. I will pay my vows to the Lord in the presence of all his people." The Psalmist sings about the moment when he will present his drink and fellowship offering to the Lord in the temple as a thanksgiving. Specifically, the Psalmist vows (116:17): "I will offer to you a thanksgiving sacrifice and call on the name of the Lord." Clearly, the thanksgiving sacrifice is a moment of tremendous joy and gratitude. It is offered as a "thank you" to the God who grants healing and blessing. Similarly, Psalm 56:12-13 presents a thanksgiving offering to God because he "delivered" him "from death." Also, Psalm 107:22 calls Israel to "offer thanksgiving sacrifices, and tell of his deeds with songs of joy."

Though not specifically called a fellowship offering, Hannah brought such an offering to the tabernacle in 1 Samuel 1. When she was barren, Hannah had prayed for a son. The Lord heard her prayer and gave her a son whom she named Samuel. When the child was weaned, she took him to the tabernacle at Shiloh. Along with the boy, she took "a three-year-old bull, an ephah of flour [about 3/5 bushel], and a skin of wine" (1 Sam. 1:24). Clearly, she intended to make a grain (involving leavened bread) and a drink offering as part of the thanksgiving offering. Since a three-year-old bull was about 800 pounds of meat that had to be eaten that same day, she intended to celebrate the birth of her son and his dedication to divine service with friends and family as well as the priestly personnel. She celebrated God's grace and blessing with a party—a thanksgiving meal.

The fellowship meal was also an occasion for covenant renewal. Psalm 50 is sung in this kind of context. When Israel assembles to praise God, the Lord comes among them. But this is not always a gracious coming. Sometimes God comes to judge those who have made a covenant with him because they have not followed the covenant (Ps. 50:5-6, 16-20). As the act of a changed heart, God calls his people to "offer a sacrifice of thanksgiving" and "pay" their "vows to the Most High" (Ps. 50:14; cf. 50:23). The fellowship meal is not only a moment of thanksgiving, but it is also a time of rededication and renewal. The worshipper makes a vow and commits himself to faithfulness before the Lord.

One of the best examples of fellowship offerings on a national level is Hezekiah's dedication of the temple in 2 Chronicles 29 and his two week celebration of the Passover in 2 Chronicles 30. On both occasions hundreds of animals were sacrificed (2 Chron. 29:31-35; 30:23-24). In particular, 19,000 animals were sacrificed to celebrate the Passover for an additional seven days. This was not because God demanded 19,000 animals as his price of grace, but rather this many animals were needed to feed the gathered assembly. The result was that "the whole assembly of Judah, the priests and the Levites, and the whole of assembly that came out of Israel, and the resident aliens who came out of the land of Israel, and the resident aliens who lived in Judah, rejoiced" (2 Chron. 30:25). The Chronicler comments (2 Chron. 30:26): "There was great joy in Jerusalem."

The Meaning of the Fellowship Meal

Several features characterize the fellowship meals of Israel. First, it is a moment of communion between God and his people. God eats with his people as the fat is burned to him. God is present at this meal. It is eaten before the Lord as if God sits at the table with the worshipper. Thus, worshippers eat with assurance, thanksgiving and confidence as they experience communion with God in this meal. God comes to the table with his people as he calls them to a table to experience his communion.

Second, it is a communal act among the covenant people of God. It is a shared offering—it is shared with God, the priests and the community (friends and family). The meal involved more meat than one single individual could possibly eat in one or two days. The ritual regulations, therefore, imposed a communal meaning on the meal. Since the sacrifice had to be eaten within two days at the most, it forced the worshipper to share the meal with others. God never intended humanity to eat alone. Rather, God eats with them and a community surrounds them as fellow-participants in the meal.

Third, it is always characterized by joy and gratitude. Without exception, the fellowship offering is a celebratory, festive occasion. It is a time of thanksgiving, dedication and renewal. The note of joy is overwhelming. It characterized all Israel's festivals. For example, Numbers 10:10 commands that "on your days of rejoicing, at your appointed festivals, and at the beginning of your months, you shall blow the trumpets" over your fellowship offerings. When Saul was crowned king "before the Lord," Israel "sacrificed offerings of well-being before the Lord" and "all the Israelites rejoiced greatly" (1 Sam. 11:15). The fellowship meal, then, was always a moment of joy and celebration. It was never characterized by sadness or guiltiness. It was the experience of communion with God and celebration of God's covenant faithfulness that generated the joy which worshippers experienced at the table.

In the Hebrew Bible the table is a communal act of communion with God characterized by joy (thanksgiving) and rededication (vow). At Solomon's inauguration Israel "ate and drank before the Lord on that day with great joy" (1 Chron. 29:22). It was not a moment of solemn, private silence. It was not an individualistic act. On the contrary, it was an interactive meal which engaged the whole community in joyous, celebrative fellowship with God.

Conclusion

Paul pointed the Corinthians to the sacrifices of Israel as a way of understanding the Lord's supper. Eating the Lord's supper is analogous to eating Israel's sacrifices. We learn from the later more about the former.[4]

The Lord's supper is a thanksgiving meal. Jesus, for example, gave thanks for the bread (Lk. 22:19; 1 Cor. 11:24) and the cup (Mk. 14:23; Matt. 26:27). The Lord's supper is a moment of gratitude. Thus, the church has historically called it a "Euchar-ist" from the Greek word which means "thanksgiving." But if it shares in the meaning of the thanksgiving meals of Israel, the Lord's supper needs to be revisioned along the lines of the those meals.

The Lord's supper should be understood as an interactive meal which engages the whole community in joyous, celebra-tive fellowship with God. If the supper is a thanksgiving meal, why is the dominant practice of the supper so silent, solemn, singular and sad? The supper is a table, not an altar. It is the experience of communion, not the search for atonement.

Heeding the admonition of Paul, we should consider the impact that the fellowship meals of Israel should have on the Lord's supper. As a thanksgiving meal, it should be celebrative and joyous. As a fellowship meal, it should be communal and interactive. As a participation in the altar, the cross, it should be the experience of grace and blessing as we eat in the presence of God. When we eat, we commune with God and with each other, and that is reason to celebrate.

Questions for Discussion

1. How do the sacrificial rituals in the Old Testament distinguish between the altar and table?

2. What is the theological meaning of the "thanksgiving sacrifice" or "fellowship meal" in the Old Testament sacrificial system? How does this inform the meaning of the Lord's supper?

3. What is the atmosphere of a "fellowship meal" in the Old Testament? Describe the mood of the table in Old Testament liturgy?

4. Which example of thanksgiving or fellowship meals did you find most significant or helpful in your understanding of its significance for the supper?

PART II.

COMMUNION IN LUKE-ACTS:
EATING WITH JESUS

4 / THE MINISTRY OF JESUS

Israel entered into covenant with God at Sinai. The covenant was "cut" at the altar through the "blood of the covenant." Through atonement God came to his people and dwelt among them. On the ground of the altar, God invited his people to the table. At Sinai, and through the fellowship offerings and covenant meals in Israel's history, God sat at table with his people in holy and celebrative communion.

The story of God at table with his people continues in the ministry of Jesus. In Jesus Christ, God comes to his people to dwell among them and make himself known. In Jesus Christ, God sits at table with his people. In the Gospel of Luke the meal stories dominate the landscape of the narrative. At every turn, Jesus is eating with different kinds of people in varied settings. According to Markus Barth, "in approximately one-fifth of the sentences in Luke's Gospel and in Acts, meals play a conspicuous role."[1] Koenig even describes eating and drinking as the "organizing principle" of Luke's story.[2] Table fellowship is a focal point of Jesus' ministry and it became a focal point of the early church.

The table ministry of Jesus is often ignored in framing our understanding of the Lord's supper. For some it seems too removed from the Last Supper and for others the Lord's supper is a highly formalized ritual unlike the tables of Jesus' ministry. However, in the Gospel of Luke the Last Supper is linked with the other tables in the narrative by language and content. The Last Supper is one meal among many, but it is also the paradigmatic meal for understanding the rest of the meals. It is the final meal in a series of meals during the ministry of Jesus. Instead of the Last Supper standing aloof from these other meals, it gives fuller meaning to them. The Last Supper interprets and gives substance to the other meals as they are understood in the theological light of that Last Supper.

"Eating with Jesus" involves three movements. First, in this chapter we will look at the meals Jesus ate with people during his ministry. In the fifth chapter we will examine the Last Supper as the so-called "institution of the Lord's supper." In the sixth chapter we will see how the early church in Acts followed Jesus and continued to eat with him through the "breaking of bread." The central text, Luke 22 where the Last Supper is described, will interpret the meals of Jesus in Luke and the meals of the early church in Acts.

The Meals with Jesus in Luke

The chart below conveniently summarizes the meals of Jesus in the Gospel of Luke.[3] The chart notes the participants in the meals, interprets the significance of each meal and identifies the key saying of Jesus at each meal which focuses the theological intent of the story. Each meal story is a theological story and it reveals something about Jesus and his mission. Table is a primary moment of teaching in the Gospel of Luke as well as a time of communion.

The first meal with Jesus in the Gospel is found in Luke 5:27-32. Jesus invited the tax collector Levi (Matthew) to follow

Luke	Meal	Participants	Significance	Teaching Moment
5:27-32	Banquet at Levi's house	Tax collectors & sinners	Evangelism	"I have come to call not the righteous, but sinners to repentance."
7:36-50	Dinner at Simon the Pharisee's house	Pharisees, guests & the sinful woman	Reconciliation	"Your sins are forgiven."
9:10-17	Breaking bread at Bethsaida	5,000 males	Mission/ service	"You give them something to eat."
10:38-42	Hospitality at the home of Martha	Disciples	Discipleship	"Mary has chosen the better part."
11:37-54	Noon meal at a Pharisee's house	Pharisees & teachers	Inner life	"You Pharisees clean the outside of the cup but inside you are full of great wickedness."
14:1-24	Sabbath dinner at a Pharisee's house	Pharisees & their friends	Invitation to all	"When you give a banquet, invite the poor, crippled, lame, and blind."
19:1-10	Hospitality at the house of Zacchaeus	Zacchaeus, the tax collector, & others	Salvation for all	"The Son of Man came to seek & save the lost."
22:7-38	Last Supper—a Passover meal	The Twelve, including Judas	Thanksgiving	"Then he took a loaf of bread and, when he had given thanks, he broke it & gave it to them."
24:13-35	Breaking bread at Emmaus	Two disciples	The Living One	Jesus was "made known to them in the breaking of the bread"
24:36-53	Supper with the disciples	The Eleven & others with them	The missionary community	"You are witnesses of these things."

him, and Levi "got up, left everything, and followed him." Levi then gathered his friends together for a "great banquet" at his house. His friends included a "large crowd of tax collectors." The Pharisees recognized this as a gathering of "tax collectors" and sinners. Levi's guests were "sinners," and the Pharisees questioned why the disciples would sit at table with such people. In response, Jesus characterized his intent as a call to repentance. He shares table fellowship with sinners in order to call them to a lifestyle change. It is a meal with evangelistic intent. As Jesus eats and drinks with sinners, he calls them into fellowship with God through repentance. His presence at the table with sinners, however, is a testimony of the goodness and grace of God who calls sinners to repentance.

It is interesting that the Pharisees question the disciples rather than Jesus. It is as if we are overhearing a conversation between religious leaders in Luke's community who question the invitation of sinners to the table. The response is that table is an evangelistic opportunity. When we invite sinners to the table, we call them to repentance and we bear witness to the gracious disposition of God to receive sinners into fellowship. The disciples of Jesus, just as Jesus himself did, must remain open to table fellowship with sinners for the sake of their healing.

The second meal with Jesus in the Gospel is found in Luke 7:36-50. While in the first story Jesus eats with sinners, in this story Jesus eats at the house of a Pharisee who is not very hospitable toward him. The Pharisee does not greet Jesus with a kiss, wash his feet or anoint his head with oil. It appears that the Pharisee sits at table with Jesus with hostile motives, but Jesus eats with him anyway. The story takes on new significance when a sinful woman (prostitute?) crashed the party and extended to Jesus the hospitality that the Pharisee refused to give. She kissed, washed and anointed Jesus' feet. The theological point of the story is evidenced in Jesus' parable about the two debtors who were forgiven their debts. The Pharisee loved little because he saw himself in little need of forgiveness, but the woman loved much because her sins were many. The words of Jesus to the woman are the climax of the story: "Your sins are forgiven."

Table with Jesus becomes an occasion of forgiveness and reconciliation. The woman and Jesus are reconciled as her sins are forgiven, but the Pharisee and the woman are not reconciled. The Pharisee is unwilling to extend grace and compassion toward this repentant sinner. God in Jesus receives the sinner, but the Pharisee does not. The significance for the disciples of Jesus is difficult to miss. Table is a place of reconciliation rather than hostility and suspicion. In the movie *Jesus of Nazareth*, Jesus tells the parable of the prodigal son (Lk. 15:11-32) in the context of a table. While contextually incorrect, theologically it is exactly the point. At the end of the parable the father invites the elder son to eat and celebrate the return of the lost son. The parable is open-ended. We do not know what the elder son did, and it is open-ended precisely to invite us to decide what we will do. Luke 7 and Luke 15 call God's people to reconciliation around a table.

The third meal with Jesus in the Gospel is found in Luke 9:10-17. This story is significant for several reasons. First, it is the only meal in Luke prior to the Last Supper (Lk. 22) where Jesus is the host. Second, it contains language that is explicitly tied to the Last Supper (he took the bread, blessed it, broke it and gave it to the disciples; Lk. 9:16 with Lk. 22:19). Third, the meal has explicit messianic overtones as the Messiah feeds his people and eats with them.

Just prior to this meal story, Jesus had sent "the twelve" out to "preach the kingdom of God and to heal" the sick (Lk. 9:1-2). Upon their return, Jesus retires with them to Bethsaida (Lk. 9:11). Between these two paragraphs, Luke injects the question which shapes the rest of the narrative. Herod the tetrarch asked: "Who is this about whom I hear such things?" The dominant question of the narrative is "who is Jesus?" The narrative answers the question in Luke 9:20 by the mouth of Peter: "The Messiah of God." Luke heightened the messianic character of this meal by placing this text prior to the confession of Jesus as the Christ (9:20) so that the hospitality (9:11), preaching, healing and feeding of his people are signs by which Peter recognizes his messianic character. The text has messianic banquet overtones and offers a context for interpreting the Lord's supper.

The meal story, then, is an identity story. It identifies Jesus as the Messiah who hosts a meal with his disciples. This is a messianic banquet as the Messiah welcomes the crowd that followed him to Bethsaida (Lk. 9:11), teaches them about the kingdom of God (Lk. 9:11) and provides their "food and lodging" (Lk. 9:12, NIV). Jesus, as Messiah, feeds the people of God in a "remote place" (Lk. 9:12, NIV), just as God did with manna in the wilderness. The table confirms Jesus' identity as God's anointed one. The meal is characterized by joy, abundance and compassion as Jesus feeds the hungry.

The chart below illustrates the connections between the feeding of the 5000 in Luke 9 and the Last Supper of Luke 22. The thematic connection indicates that Luke intended his community to read Luke 9 in the light of the table in the kingdom of God. This meal is the meal of the kingdom, just as Luke 22 is the meal of the kingdom and the Lord's supper is the meal of the kingdom. All of them anticipate the fullness of the Messianic banquet in the new heaven and new earth.

The key saying in the text is found in Luke 9:13. In the face of an overwhelming crowd of people, Jesus instructed his disciples to "give them something to eat." The disciples are called to service. The table has a missional dimension; it reflects the mission of God to commune with his people at table. As LaVerdiere comments, "The mission of the Twelve and of the church was to continue Jesus' proclamation of the gospel of the kingdom of God as well as Jesus' offer of hospitality at the table

Topic	Luke 9	Luke 22
Kingdom language	Spoke about the kingdom	Fulfillment in the kingdom
Twelve	Twelve apostles/baskets	Twelve tribes/apostles
Israel/Exodus/Wilderness	Manna in the wilderness	Exodus material
Disciples disputing	Who's the greatest	Who's the greatest
Reclining (at table)	Table etiquette	Table etiquette
Liturgical formula	Took, blessed, broke, gave	Took, blessed, broke, gave
Jesus as host	Host in the wilderness	Host at the Passover
Hospitality (lodging)	Providing hospitality	Accepting hospitality
Apostolic mission	Traveling missionaries	Judging the tribes
Eating a meal	Loaves and fishes	Passover lamb
Service	Disciples serve	Jesus serves

of the kingdom."[4] When the original Christian community read Luke 9:16, it certainly reminded them of their consistent practice of the Lord's supper. They remembered God's provision for them in Christ and the presence of Christ as the host of their supper.

The fourth meal with Jesus in the Gospel is found in Luke 10:38-42. Strikingly, for first century Palestinian culture, a woman welcomed Jesus to her home where usually one is welcomed by a male host. Jesus enters the home of a woman named Martha. Equally extraordinary in this setting is the fact that another woman is described as a disciple—she "sat at the Lord's feet and listened" to his teaching (literally, "heard his word" as one who spoke the "word of God," cf. Lk. 5:1). Jesus transcends social barriers and prejudices by calling women as his disciples and staying in the home of a woman.

The story emphasizes the female gender, the tasks of ministry (*diakonein* in 10:40) and the supreme value of discipleship (hearing the word of the Lord). How are these themes interrelated? LaVerdiere suggests that Mary reflects the "development in Christian communities, which accepted women as disciples in the full sense."[5] There is always the danger of relegating women to tasks of ministry (e.g., serving tables, though they are not permitted to serve tables in many corporate settings for worship at the Lord's table) rather than recognizing their full status as disciples. The story prioritizes discipleship over ministry and suggests that only focused attention on the word of the Lord gives meaning to table ministry. The table, therefore, cannot be separated from the word. The table gains its significance and meaning from the word. The word must shape the table and the table must display authentic discipleship. Women may serve the table as authentic disciples who are attentive to the word of the Lord.

The fifth meal with Jesus in the Gospel is found in Luke 11:37-54. For a second time, Jesus sits at table in the home of a Pharisee. While the previous meal story was about reconciliation (Lk. 7), this one is about internal purity and authentic righteousness occasioned by Jesus' failure to "wash" (literally, "dip" as a form of *baptizein*, to baptize) before eating. The concern for ceremonial purity among the Pharisees is renowned. They meticulously followed the technicalities of external observance. Jesus defies the normal conventions of external purity as he sits "unbaptized" at a table where he knew he was expected to wash first. The table becomes a teaching moment for the Pharisees present, and the teaching insults them (Lk. 11:45).

At the table, Jesus condemns the Pharisees for their self-righteousness in three ways. First, they are more concerned about external purity through ceremonial observance than internal purity. While they are clean on the outside, they are "full of greed and wickedness" on the inside. His solution is that they give their wealth to the poor ("alms") rather than concentrating on the externals which cannot cleanse the soul. Second, he condemns their minute attention to tithing while at the same time they "neglect justice and the love of God." They focused on the external righteousness of tithing without cultivating the heart of God in their inner life. Third, he condemns their search for preeminence. They love the important seats in the synagogues and respectful greetings in the marketplace. No doubt they also took the best places at the table.

Each of these condemnations addresses the significance of the interior life for the disciple. Greed and pride have no place at the table. Disciples should use the table to share with the poor, to focus on God's justice and love, and humble themselves among the people of God. The table is the place where communion should reflect divine values—God's preference for the poor, justice and love, and humility. The table is not about external technicalities. Jesus' disciples should cultivate those divine values in their lives.

The sixth meal with Jesus in the Gospel is found in Luke 14:1-24. Jesus ate a sabbath supper in the home of a Pharisee. The Pharisees were "watching him closely" with hostile intent. They tested Jesus to see if he would heal on the sabbath, which he did. They sought the "places of honor" at the table and rejoiced in their status. Jesus recommended a different table etiquette—choose the lower seat and wait for the host to move you to a more honorable seat. But it is not merely etiquette; it is about humility. The table is a place for humility, not pride. When disciples gather at a table, it is a time for humility as disciples seek the lower seats.

The guests' self-centered focus on honor and pride occasioned two "dinner" parables by Jesus (Lk. 14:12-14 and Lk. 14:16-24). Jesus turns pride on its head. Instead of taking pride in inviting the most renowned of your community and seating them in the places of honor, "invite the poor, the crippled, the lame, and the blind" (Lk. 14:13). Instead of glorying in our own expectation of eating in the kingdom of God as God's chosen ones, God will receive, according to Jesus, "the poor, the crippled, the blind, and the lame" (Lk. 14:21).

What should the table in the kingdom of God look like? The Pharisaic expectation was that the "righteous," the honored and the wealthy would sit at God's table in the kingdom. Instead, Jesus sees the poor, the blind and the lame at his table. In the light of this story, Willimon addresses this question to the church: "Today, when people look at the church and ask it, 'Are you Christ's body, or shall we look for another?' the only true test to which the church can refer is that of our Lord himself. We have to point them to our table, to that conglomeration of sick, hurting people, with the nobodies up at the head table eating like somebodies, with the outcasts invited in and being filled with good things. If this isn't church, what is?"[6]

The seventh meal with Jesus in the Gospel is found in Luke 19:1-10. While a meal is not explicitly mentioned in this story, it is present through the idea of hospitality as Jesus welcomed (same verb as in Lk. 10:38) and stays (*katalusai* in Lk. 19:7 means to show hospitality) in Zaccheus' home. The table in this story is associated with "justice, concern for the poor and salvation."[7] Table fellowship is an occasion for the experience of salvation by Zaccheus as he commits himself to repay those he has cheated and give half of his wealth to the poor. Eating with Jesus confronts us with the compassion, justice and salvation of God, and calls us to discipleship. To eat at the Lord's table is to share his values and to pursue compassion and justice in our communities.

But the story also bears witness to the self-righteousness of the people. "All who saw" Jesus' gracious encounter with the tax collector Zaccheus questioned his willingness to accept the hospitality of a "sinner." This was not simply the questioning of a few Pharisees, but the general attitude of the people. Jesus demonstrates a compassion that is lacking among the people. He is willing to receive sinners. Indeed, he "came to seek out and to save" sinners. The table is a place where Jesus receives sinners and is willing to eat with them. Salvation is experienced at table with Jesus.

Theological Meaning

Luke is a narrator. He tells stories rather than writing didactic prose. Through the stories he inculcates the values which he wants his community to embrace. The meal stories have theological meaning for Luke's community, and they are stories that should shape meals in the early church. The table during Jesus' ministry should shape the table in the church because the table of Jesus is the table of the kingdom. The table of Jesus' ministry continues in the church when his disciples gather at table. Jesus' table etiquette is kingdom etiquette, and Lord's supper is the Lord's kingdom table.

Fundamentally, "the presence of the Messiah among the people marks the beginning of a festive time as the common meal with sinners, the feeding of thousands of hungry people, the banquet and dance arranged for the prodigal who has returned home—such events loudly proclaim, 'Now is the day of salvation' (2 Corinthians 6:2). The day of great joy for all the people (cf., e.g., Luke 2:14: 13:17) has dawned."[8]

The table announces the presence of the kingdom. It announces that "today" salvation has come to the world as God communes with his people at table. It is a Jubilee festival. Jesus came to seek and to save the lost, and also to eat with them. Jubilee includes shared meals between the Messiah and his people. "Luke," according to Kodell, "makes this a major theme, portraying Jesus as the prophet whose pattern of eating and drinking with sinners is an acted parable proclaiming God's offer of life to all."[9] Salvation, and its attendant joy, are experienced when we sit at table with Jesus.

The Jubilee motif, articulated in Luke 4:16-19, not only invests the table with great joy, but it also calls the disciples of Jesus to embrace all those who are invited to his table. The table is inclusive and intentionally includes the poor, blind and oppressed. The table reaches across all socio-economic, racial and gender barriers as it unites lost humanity at one table. Jesus modeled the acceptance of who would come to the table. Jesus modeled the invitation of all to the table as he welcomed Pharisee and tax collector, rich and poor, male and female. This inclusiveness testifies to the socio-ethical character of the table as a uniting moment in the kingdom of God. All are sinners and all are accepted.

What occurs at the table is a proclamation of Jesus Christ's goodness, of his association with sinners and his full solidarity with them – of all that is most clearly demonstrated in his death on the cross, between two criminals. Love for this Christ can be shown only when the neighbors chosen by Christ are gladly accepted.[10] As Kodell comments, "those who share the eucharistic table must decide whether they are willing to make the commitment their fellowship with the Lord implies."[11] Jesus welcomes all, and so should the church of God.

But the meals with Jesus in Luke are not only about the table of the Lord in the church. They also point to the eschatological messianic banquet in the coming kingdom of God. It is anticipated in the feeding of the 5000 (Lk. 9:10-17), described as an eschatological event where people from all over the world will join Abraham at the banquet (Lk. 13:28-30), regarded as a blessed event (Lk. 14:15-24) and promised at the last supper (Lk. 22:28-30). The table of the Lord in the church, just as the meals in the ministry of Jesus, is a harbinger of that future banquet. There Jesus will provide a festive meal, dwell with us and serve us at his table in his kingdom (Lk. 12:35-38). At that meal there will be no distinction between rich and poor, slave and free, Jew and Gentile, or male and female. The one people of God will inherit the earth and enjoy the table of God forever.

Conclusion

In Jesus Christ, God continued his relationship with Israel. Just as God ate with Israel through sacrificial meals, so God comes in Jesus Christ to eat with his people. This time, however, he comes in the flesh to eat, and in his eating he testifies to the kingdom of God. In the Gospel of Luke that testimony is most fully articulated at table.

The kingdom of God at the table is a joyous celebration because it is the presence of salvation. To eat with Jesus is to experience redemption and acceptance. Jesus meets sinners at the table, calls them to repentance and communes with them. The table bears witness to redemption.

The kingdom of God at the table is inclusive because it welcomes all to the table. It includes females as well as males, slaves as well as free, poor as well as rich. It is deliverance for the oppressed and relief to the poor. The table bears witness to community.

The kingdom of God at the table anticipates the coming full reign of God where we will dwell with God on the new earth and eat at the banquet table. The table bears witness to hope. Table fellowship is a symbol of community fellowship. The table designates a special relationship between those who sit at the same table. Jesus eats with sinners and tax collectors (Lk. 5:27-32; 7:34; 15:2). He goes to the house of Zaccheus (Lk. 19:1-9). The table is for the oppressed, handicapped and disenfranchised (Lk. 7:22; 14:12-14). A banquet is thrown for the returning prodigal son (Lk. 15:11-32). Will the elder brother join in the celebration meal? Will the Pharisees have table fellowship with tax collectors in the kingdom of God? Will the contemporary Christians welcome all to the table? As Barth comments, "Whoever considers those table companions of Jesus too bad, too base, too little, too far removed from salvation to be met at Jesus' side does not see, accept, and believe Jesus as he really is. Whoever feels too good and too noble to be found in that company cannot sit at the Lord's Table."[12]

Questions for Discussion

1. What do you think is the value of studying the meals of Jesus during his ministry? Does this relate to the Lord's supper in any significant way?

2. Describe the meaning of "table fellowship" in the ministry of Jesus. How should this shape our understanding and practice of the supper?

3. Which meal story in the ministry of Jesus did you find most significant for understanding the supper?

4. What is the relationship between the feeding of the 5000 in Luke 9 and the Lord's supper?

5 / THE LAST SUPPER

The most familiar text regarding the Lord's supper is probably one of the synoptic treatments of the Last Supper (Mk. 14, Matt. 26, Lk. 22). The accounts of the three synoptic gospels have much in common, but there are significant differences in emphases. Luke is the most unique account of the three as it is twice as long as Mark and Matthew. In addition to the actual words of institution (Lk. 22:17-20) which are paralleled in Mark and Matthew, Luke supplies an introduction and conclusion which the others do not (Lk. 22:15-16, 24-30). Conse-quently, and in light of Luke's emphasis on meals in his Gospel and in Acts, I have chosen to focus on Luke's telling of the Last Supper.

In the Gospel of Luke, the Last Supper is one of Jesus' meals with his disciples and others. Indeed, even in this last meal, he shares table fellowship with a sinner (Judas) just as he had in his ministry. This Last Supper should not be disconnect-ed from the previous meals in the Gospel or the subsequent meals in Acts. The institution of the Lord's supper is the inter-pretation of what meals mean in the Christian community, and Luke has already been shaping that interpretation by his meal

motif throughout the Gospel. Further, he will assume this interpretation when he describes the practice of the primitive
church in Acts. Consequently, all that has gone before in the
Gospel should inform our understanding of the Lord's supper,
but the Last Supper is the paradigmatic interpretation of the
meaning of this covenant meal in the church of God.

The Passover Context of the Last Supper

According to Luke 22, the new covenant meal was instituted during the last Passover supper. On the day that the
"Passover lamb had to be sacrificed," Jesus told Peter and John
to prepare a place to eat the Passover (Lk. 22:7-8). Whatever
the relationship of this text is to the Gospel of John where Jesus
dies as the Passover lamb (cf. John 19:36 with Exodus 13:46
and Numbers 9:12)—and it is a difficult problem that has generated many solutions[1]—Luke's narrative clearly identifies the
meal as a Passover event. The disciples "prepared the Passover
meal" (Lk. 22:13) and Jesus declared his eagerness "to eat this
Passover with" them before he suffered (Lk. 22:15).

Luke directly links the old covenant Passover with the new
covenant meal. Jesus ate this Passover with the anticipation that
he would eat with his disciples again in the kingdom of God.
Specifically, he told his disciples that he "eagerly desired to eat
this Passover with you before I suffer, for I tell you, I will not
eat it until it is fulfilled in the kingdom of God" (Lk. 22:15-16).
What Jesus intends to eat in the future is the fulfillment of the
Passover itself. The Passover supper finds its fulfillment in the
kingdom of God where they would eat and drink at Jesus' table
in his kingdom (Lk. 22:30). It is not simply the bread and wine
that fulfill the Passover typology, but eating the meal. The meal,
rather than simply bread and wine, is the Lord's supper as it fulfills the Passover.

Luke places this new covenant meal on the trajectory of
redemptive history where the goal is the eschatological com-

munity of God in the heavenly kingdom. Jesus will eat and drink with the disciples again when the kingdom comes (Lk. 22:18). The fullness of kingdom is the reign of God in the eschaton, the new heaven and new earth (cf. parable in Lk. 19:11-27). However, Luke also believes that in the person of Jesus, who exorcises demons and raises the dead, the kingdom is already present (Lk. 11:20), and that Pentecost was the inauguration of restored Israel when Jesus ascended to the throne of David (Acts 1:6; 2:29-35 with Lk. 1:30-33). The kingdom of God is already and not yet; it is present but yet future. The Passover is fulfilled in both the church and in the future messianic banquet.

Thus, the fulfillment in Luke 22 has a dual import: it is fulfillment in the new covenant meal of the inaugurated kingdom (the church) as well as the eschatological banquet. When the church eats this meal, it eats the new covenant Passover (or thanksgiving meal) and it does so with the expectation of eschatological victory. It eats in the light of the resurrected Lord who has conquered death and will remove the disgrace of his people in the new heaven and the new earth (Isa. 25:6-9). The supper is a meal shared with the risen Lord (cf. Lk. 24:30, 35). It is eaten in the presence of Christ who, as the risen Lord, sits as the host of the meal. We eat the meal "with" Christ (Matt. 26:29).

Since the Passover anticipated the Lord's supper and the Lord's supper was instituted in the context of a Passover meal, it is important to understand the Passover in order to fully appreciate the theological meaning of the Lord's supper. While the specifics of the Passover meal at the time of Jesus are uncertain, it is generally agreed that the Passover was similar to the outline below.

The Passover Meal at the Time of Jesus[2]

Afternoon: The Slaughter of the Lamb.

Evening: The Passover Meal

1. Preliminary Course:
   Blessing of festival day spoken over First Cup of Wine
   Dish of green herbs, bitter herbs and fruit sauce
   Serving of meal and mixing of second cup of wine

2. Passover Liturgy
   The Passover narrative (*haggadah*)
   Singing of Psalm 113 (the little *hallel*)
   Second cup of wine

3. Main Meal
   Grace spoken over bread
   Meal of roasted lamb, unleavened bread, bitter herbs
   Grace spoken over third cup of wine (cup of blessing)

4. Conclusion
   Singing of Psalms 114-118 (the great *hallel*)
   Grace spoken over fourth cup of wine

Night: Watching and Remembrance

[handwritten margin note: Sounds like thanksgiving dinner]

The *haggadah* is the homily of the Passover liturgy. The host, such as the father in a family or Jesus in Luke's setting, rehearses the redemptive story, interprets it and applies its significance for the participants. The content of the *haggadah* probably varied considerably, but the contemporary standard form is derived from the Mishnah.

The *haggadah* remembered the Exodus and the hasty flight of Israel from Egypt. It recalled how Israel began in the loins of Abraham who was a "wandering Aramean" (cf. Deut. 26:5-11). It recalled how God raised up Moses to deliver his people from Egyptian bondage. It called the people of God to remember their salvation and respond to that memory with celebrative praise. The Mishnaic haggadah concludes in this manner:

> Therefore are we bound to give thanks, to praise, to glorify, to honor, to exalt, to extol, and to bless him who wrought all these wonders for our fathers and for us. He brought us out from bondage to freedom, from sorrow to gladness, and from mourning to a Festival-day, and from darkness to great light, and from servitude to redemption; so let us say before him the "Hallelujah."

The Passover is a memorial characterized by praise, joy and thanksgiving. The Passover does not memorialize the Exodus as a kind of dirge or funerary remembrance. On the contrary, it is a celebration of God's redemption. It evokes praise and joy. Unfortunately, the popular conception of the Passover is tainted by the solemnity and sadness of the depiction of the Passover in Charlton Heston's *Ten Commandments*. But this offers a distorted picture. The Passover was filled with anticipation of the coming Messiah as he was expected to make his appearance at the festival. It celebrated God's redemption. The Passover is always a joyous event (cf. 2 Chron. 30:21-27; 35:16-19).

Further, the "memorial" aspect of the Passover is not merely a rehearsal of a past event. Rather, it is the present participation of the celebrant in that past event. To eat the Passover meal is to re-experience the past event in the present as if the celebrants were present at the Red Sea themselves. To "remember" the Exodus in the Passover is to experience it anew, that is, to experience the redemption anew. Consequently, as Israel prepared to enter the promised land, Moses could speak to that generation as if they themselves had been brought out of Egypt when it was their fathers who had actually been redeemed on that Passover night (Deuteronomy 16:1). To "remember" is no

[margin note: Praise is joyful, a result of celebration.]

mere cognitive event. It is to experience the redemptive presence of God again, just as their ancestors did on that first night. Luke's narrative closely resembles the Passover liturgy. The chart below identifies the resemblance (with a little help from Matthew).

The Passover	The Last Supper
The *Haggadah*	Luke 22:15-16 – Interpretation
First/Second Cup of Wine	Luke 22:17 – Cup
Breaking of the Bread	Luke 22:19 – Bread
Passover Meal	Luke 22:20 – After Supper
Third/Fourth Cup of Wine	Luke 22:20 – Cup
Singing	Matthew 26:30 – Singing
Prayer	Luke 22:40 — Prayer

In effect, Jesus eats this last Passover with his disciples, but he reinterprets its meaning in the light of the coming kingdom. It is a Passover meal that anticipates its fulfillment in the kingdom of God. In this Passover meal Jesus points his disciples to a new Exodus and the experience of a new table, a table in the kingdom of God. The Passover and the Lord's supper are not two different things, but rather the Lord's supper is a fulfillment, an enhancement, of the Passover where the climactic redemptive work of God is experienced at Jesus' table.

The Institution of the New Covenant Meal

The traditional heart of the Last Supper text is Luke 22:19-20, which is the bread and wine liturgy.

Then he took a loaf of bread, and when he had given thanks, he broke it and gave it to them, saying, "This is my body, which is given for you. Do this in remembrance of me." And he did the same with the cup after supper, saying, "This cup that is poured out for you is the new covenant in my blood."

Unfortunately, these words have occasioned considerable controversy in the history of the church. The church has debated the meaning of "this is my body" and "this is my blood" for centuries. By the middle of the sixteenth century—and ever since—Roman Catholics interpreted this in terms of transubstantiation, Lutherans in terms of consubstantiation, Anabaptists (Mennonites, Baptists, Churches of Christ, for example) in terms of symbolism and Reformed theology (Presbyterians [and Anglicans], for example) in terms of spiritual ("real") presence. This tension has divided Catholicism from Protestantism and then divided Protestants among themselves. What should unite Christians, that is, the one table, has divided them.

Roman Catholics believe that "is" means that the bread has become the body and the wine has become the blood of Christ. The substance of the bread (wine) has changed into the substance of the body (blood) even though it looks like and tastes like bread (wine). Lutherans also believe that "is" refers to the literal substance of the body and blood of Christ, but they maintain that the substance of the bread and wine remain as well. The body and blood of Christ is substantially available in, with, and under the bread and wine. Catholics and Lutherans both emphasize the substance of the body and blood as a genuine communal feast whereby Christians are nourished through participation in the substance of the body and blood.

Anabaptists, however, stress the symbolism of the term "is." The bread (wine) represents or symbolizes the body (blood). The bread (wine) is not literally the body (blood) of Christ since the body of Christ has ascended into heaven and sits at the right of hand of God. Reformed theologians also believe that the bread (wine) represents the body (blood), but they affirm that something more than mere symbolism is present. While the bread does not communicate to us the actual, physical substance of the body of Christ, it does genuinely communicate to us the spiritual reality of Christ's presence and saving work. Calvin described this spiritual communion as the Holy Spirit lifting us up into the heavenly places to spiritually feed on Christ through the bread and wine.

On one hand, this discussion is healthy. It reminds us that there is something mysterious at work at the table of the Lord. The identification of the bread (wine) with body (blood) is critical to the experience of the table, though the exact nature of this identification is cloaked in debate. But the debate evokes a sense of mystery as we sense our understanding is limited and distorted. God is at work at the table through the bread and wine. The table, then, is an occasion of awe and reverence.

On the other hand, the debate focuses attention on only one aspect of the presence of Christ at the table. The identity of the bread and wine with the body and blood of Christ serves the function of pointing us to the atoning work of Christ and our experience of the benefits of that work. The functional identity reminds us of what Christ has done for us. It serves our memory, as discussed below in more detail. But the presence of Christ is not so much in or about the bread (wine) as much as it is about his presence at the table as host. Christ is the host and he is present as a fellow-participant in the meal. We eat and drink with Christ at his table in his kingdom (Lk. 22:30). Christ sits at the table with us rather than primarily locating himself in the bread and wine. The bread and wine evoke the memory of Christ's work, but the table is the presence of Christ as one who eats and drinks with us.

The words of institution, however, emphasize that this covenant meal is focused on remembering the work of God in Christ. Just like the Passover, the new covenant meal is a memorial of God's work in redemptive history. While the Passover remembered the Exodus, the new covenant meal remembers the gospel events, the death and resurrection of Jesus. As a gospel meal, it actualizes the work of God for the community. The saving work of God is not simply a past memory, but a present reality through the covenant meal. It actualizes the reality of God's salvation for us now, just as the annual Passover reactualized the Exodus for Israel throughout its history.

The supper remembers the atoning work of Christ. The believer experiences anew the redemptive communion that God worked through the blood of the new covenant and the sacrificial offering of the body of Christ. The expiatory work of the body and blood of Jesus removes sin and enables the establishment of a covenant meal where communion is enjoyed. Luke's language reflects the influence of both Exodus 24:8 (covenant in blood) and Jeremiah 31:31 (new covenant). This language, in connection with the Passover context, establishes the covenantal character of this meal. There is a strong continuity with the old covenant meals (including thanksgiving meals and Passovers), but there is also a redemptive-historical fulfillment of the old in the new. The type has been fulfilled and taken to a new level, but that fulfillment in the Lord's supper anticipates an eschatological fulfillment when the kingdom of God fully arrives.

The words of institution are couched in altar language. They are the language of Old Testament sacrificial offerings. Christ gives his body for us, just as sacrificial offerings were gifts (cf. Heb. 5:1-2; 9:9). Christ pours out his blood, just as sacrificial blood was poured at the altar (cf. Lev. 4:7). The point is not that Christ is sacrificed again every time disciples eat and drink, but that every time disciples eat and drink they experience the mystery of the altar. They participate in the altar by communing in its benefits. But those benefits are experienced at a table and not at an altar.

We must distinguish between the altar and the table. The altar is the cross of Christ, but the table is the Lord's supper. The two should not be confused, but neither should they be disconnected. At the table we remember the altar and share in the altar's benefits, but the table should not be identified with the altar. The table remembers the altar by enjoying the communion secured by the altar. The table is the experience of peace and communion, which is celebrated with joy and thanksgiving. The altar is remembered and re-experienced in this communion, but it is not experienced as sadness but as good news (gospel). The fruit of the altar is the table, and the table is where we sit with Christ as we enjoy the benefits of the altar.

The Meaning of the Supper Applied

While both Matthew and Mark conclude the Passover meal with a hymn and move quickly to the Garden of Gethsemane, Luke dwells on the experience of the table a bit longer. Luke 22:24-30 is unique in parallel with Mark 14 and Matthew 26.

> A dispute also arose among them as to which of them was to be regarded as the greatest. And he said, "The kings of the Gentiles lord it over them; and those in authority over them are called benefactors. But not so with you; rather the greatest among you must become like the youngest, and the leader like one who serves. For who is greater, one who is at the table or the one who serves? Is it not the one at table? But I am among you as one who serves.
>
> You are those who have stood by me in my trials; and I confer [literally, "to confer by executing a covenant"] on you, just as my Father has conferred [literally, "conferred by executing a covenant"] on me, a kingdom, so that you may eat and drink at my table in my kingdom, and you will sit on the thrones judging the twelve tribes of Israel.

The saying of Jesus is not unique to Luke. It appears in Matthew 20:20-28 and Mark 10:35-45 where James and John seek the right and left hand of Jesus' throne in the coming kingdom. It generated a dispute among the disciples about who would be the greatest in the kingdom. However, Matthew and Mark point to the death of Christ as the supreme expression of greatness as Christ served humanity by giving his life as a ransom. "The Son of Man came not to be served but to serve, and to give his life as a ransom for many" (Mk. 10:45; cf. Matt. 20:28). Luke points to something else; he points to Christ's table service. Luke recontextualizes both the dispute about greatness and the supreme expression of this greatness as servanthood in the setting of the table rather than the altar (cross).

It seems rather odd and almost incredulous that the disciples would argue about greatness in the context of the altar language of the words of institution. When Jesus has just spoken about his death and his betrayal by one of the disciples, the disciples debate their relative positions in the coming kingdom. Perhaps kingdom language evoked this debate. Twice Jesus spoke of the coming kingdom (Lk. 22:16, 18). The picture of the coming kingdom engendered selfishness and pride in the disciples instead of humility and gratitude. They focused on themselves instead of the sacrifice of Christ. They sought position and status instead of ministry and service.

In response, Jesus contrasts his kingdom with the kingdoms of the Gentiles. While their kings seek control, power and authority as they dominate and rule their subjects, those who sit on the throne in the kingdom of God are not so oriented. They do not seek control, power and authority. On the contrary, they imitate the servanthood of Jesus.

At the Last Supper, Jesus was not simply "at the table." He served the table. The word Luke uses is *diakonon* (verb form of the term deacon or servant). The word primarily refers to those who wait on tables. Jesus did not come to be served, but to serve. In the context of the table, Jesus is a servant, that is, he waited on the table at the Passover meal. Jesus was not only the host, but the waiter. Indeed, as we know from John's Gospel, Jesus fully embraced the role of servant by washing the disciple's feet. When the pride of the disciples would not permit them to wash each other's feet, Jesus, though he was Lord and Teacher, picked up the towel and basin and washed the feet of his disciples to show the full extent of his love (John 13:1-20). The host, the king, became a waiter, a servant. This king does not rule with control, authority and power, but he leads through service. Even though it was his table, Jesus served his disciples.

Unfortunately, the significance of this service is sometimes undermined by attributing this ministry to the incarnational function of the Son. "Of course," some might say, "the Son was servant while on the earth, but now he is Lord and rules with power and authority." This tends to discount the servanthood of Jesus as merely conditioned by his humanity. But this misses the point that Jesus is the incarnation of God and reveals the heart of God through that incarnation.

Servanthood is the heart of God. God served humanity by creating them. God serves them in redemption, particularly through the incarnation and death of Jesus Christ. But the servanthood of Jesus as the revealer of God is best illustrated in Luke by Jesus' relationship to the table. The incarnate Son served his disciples at the table, but this service is no mere momentary blip on the screen. Rather, it is the intention of the Son to serve humanity at the table in the new heaven and new earth. In the eschaton the Son, though Master, will serve his servants at the table when God spreads the messianic banquet for his people. "Blessed are those slaves whom the master finds alert when he comes," Jesus says, "truly I tell you, he will fasten his belt and have them sit down to eat, and he will come and serve (diakonesei) them" (Lk. 12:37).

God conferred on Jesus a kingdom through covenant and Jesus ruled this kingdom through service. In the same way Jesus confers a kingdom on his disciples as he seats them on thrones to judge the twelve tribes of Israel. However, their rule is not about control, power and authority. Rather, they should lead through service as Jesus led.

The table is not about power, control or authority. It is not about clerical authority. It is not about gender prerogatives. It is about mutual service and ministry. The table is where we serve each other. The table embodies the mutual love and respect we have for each other as we sit at the table with the host who served us all.

Unfortunately, the table has become the locus of hierarchical positioning. In some traditions, only clergy may serve the table. In some traditions, only men may serve the table. But disciples sit at the table as servants, not authoritarians or hierarchicalists. We sit at the table to serve each other, not to dominate each other. When we use the table to promote hierarchical values, we undermine its intention to unite the people of God in mutual service. It seems rather strange that clerics can assume the role of host when Jesus is the host of the table, and it seems odd that the only table women cannot serve in our churches is the Lord's table. All disciples are called to imitate Jesus by serving the table and to deny any saint the opportunity to serve the table is to deny that one the opportunity to imitate Jesus.

When disciples sit at the table together with Jesus as the host, they commit themselves to imitate him. They commit themselves to be servants. Just as Jesus served us, even to the extent of sacrificing his life, so disciples commit to serve each other as Jesus served them. We cannot sit at table with fellow disciples and then fail to serve them when they are in need. We cannot commune with each other at the table and then fail to commune with each other in the sharing of our possessions to meet each other's needs. To sit at the table and deny ministry to another is to undermine the meaning of the gospel. The table must extend beyond the worship assembly as it shapes the ministry of God's people throughout the week.

Table service is a symbol for community service. Table etiquette demanded that at formal dinners there should be servants to serve. Feet were washed by servants, the table was served by servants, and the tables were cleared by servants. In Luke this service is shared by the community as a whole for the community as a whole. The disciples are fellow-servants, and Jesus himself is a servant at the table (Lk. 22:25-27). The servants are served at the table of the Lord by Jesus himself in the eschatological banquet (Lk. 12:35-37). The table, as much as anything else in the community of God, should embody this mutual service.

Conclusion

Jesus instituted a supper where his people might remember him. His model for this supper was the sacrificial meals of the Hebrew Bible. In particular, he instituted his own supper in the context of a Passover meal. Jesus instituted a meal, not just bread and wine. The meal (in Luke, cup-bread-supper-cup) fulfills the Passover in the kingdom of God and anticipates the full messianic banquet in the new heaven and new earth. If the Old Testament festivals involved a full meal (like the Passover) and the future messianic banquet involves a full meal, the new covenant meal, the Lord's supper, also involves a full meal.

Yet, the focus of this meal is realized memory. It is not simply a cognitive reflection on the past, but the renewed experience of the redemptive work of God in the present. The table is the experience of genuine spiritual fellowship. The redemptive benefits of the altar are actualized in the present through the table. The memory of the past event is actually realized in the present as the people of God commune with Jesus at the table.

"Table," moreover, is not simply about vertical communion with God. On the contrary, to sit at the table is to commit to serving those who sit at the table with you. It is to participate in the community of faith. It is a moment of mutual commitment and mutual service. The table involves communion between God and his people and among the people of God. God in Jesus serves the table and at the table we serve each other.

Questions for Discussion

1. How does the Passover shape the meaning and practice of the supper?

2. What is the meaning of "is" in the phrases "this is my body" and "this is my blood"? Mere symbolism? Authentic communion? Physical substance?

3. What is the significance of the "altar" language in the institution of the Lord's supper? How does the table relate to the altar?

4. How does Jesus apply the meaning of the table for his disputing disciples? What are the implications of "servanthood" for the contemporary practice of the supper?

6 / THE PRIMITIVE CHURCH IN ACTS

In the Gospel of Luke, Jesus compassionately "broke bread" with five thousand males as he proclaimed "the kingdom of God" to them (Lk. 9:11, 16). As Jesus ate his last Passover with his disciples, he "broke" bread with them while at the same time declaring that he would not eat this meal with them again until the kingdom of God had come (Lk. 22:16, 19). And, then, after his resurrection, Jesus "breaks bread" with two disciples at Emmaus (Lk. 24:30) and the church continues to "break bread" as a community in the book of Acts (Acts 2:42, 46; 20:7, 11).

To understand what Luke intends by "breaking bread" we must read the text as original readers in the context of an existing church community, and we must read the narrative intratextually. That is, we must read the text as a unit and from within its own frame of reference. Luke provides the clues for understanding "breaking of bread." The dominant, and overriding clue, is the institution of the Lord's supper itself. There the liturgical pattern is established which reflected the language current in the church of his day: (1) he took bread; (2) he blessed it; (3) he broke it; and (4) he gave it. "Breaking bread" has Christological significance for Luke. It is Luke's phrase for the Lord's supper; it is a meal where Jesus hosts the table.

Luke understands "breaking of bread" as the fulfillment of the Passover and he understands that the disciples sit at the table of the Lord. Indeed, the Lord is both victim and host of this table by which he bequeaths the kingdom to his disciples, just as the Father had bequeathed it to him. Together, then, in the kingdom, the disciples and Jesus anticipate eating and drinking anew this meal. Luke tells us that they will "break bread" again as a community.

The Gospel of Luke, then, in the meal stories of Jesus, the feeding of the five thousand, and the institution of the Lord's supper at Passover defines the meaning of "breaking bread." When Acts refers to the "breaking of bread" the readers remember Luke's stories in his Gospel. "Breaking bread" is not a new idea in Acts 2:42. On the contrary, Luke has already introduced the theme and need not explain its meaning. Readers understand that the phrase comes from the institution of the Lord's supper and the meal stories in the Gospel. It means to eat with Jesus.

Luke-Acts tells three stories about disciples "breaking bread" after the resurrection of Jesus.[1] The first involves two disciples who break bread with Jesus in Emmaus (Lk. 24:30). The second describes the Jerusalem church as a community which broke bread in their homes (Acts 2:42-47). The third describes a gathering of disciples in Troas which broke bread together (Acts 20:7-12).

Breaking Bread in Emmaus

During the Last Supper Jesus promised that he would not eat and drink with his disciples again until the kingdom of God had come (Lk. 22:16, 18). Three days later, on the first day of the week, Jesus is eating with his disciples (Lk. 24:30, 42-43). In some sense the kingdom of God had come though it had not arrived in its fullest sense.

The kingdom of God had arrived in the resurrection of Jesus, which is an event from the future. The resurrection of Jesus is the first fruit of a coming harvest. Jesus is the firstborn from the dead and his resurrection guarantees the resurrection of his disciples. The presence of the firstborn Jesus is the presence of the future kingdom. In this sense, the kingdom came on the first day of the week after the Last Supper. In this sense Jesus kept his promise to eat and drink with his disciples when the kingdom of God had come.

To eat and drink with Jesus, then, is to experience the presence of the kingdom and hope. The presence of the living Christ at the table of the kingdom is the guarantee of our own future resurrection. The table transforms death into life, despair into hope.

This was the experience of the disciples themselves on that first Easter. The previous Friday had destroyed their hope. Calvary was, in their eyes, a defeat. The cross ended the life of the one whom they had hoped was the deliverer of Israel (Lk. 24:21). They still believed he was a good man, a miracle-worker, even a prophet. But they had lost hope that he was the Messiah.

As two of the disciples walked from Jerusalem to Emmaus on that first day of the week, they returned home as dejected and defeated people. They had even heard reports about an empty tomb and heard the women testify about the appearance of angels. They had heard the rumors that Jesus had been raised from the dead. But they did not believe them. They were still a dejected and defeated pair as they traveled to Emmaus.

As they walked, Jesus joined them on their journey, though "their eyes were kept from recognizing him" (Lk. 24:16). Apparently, God had covered their eyes so that they would not recognize Jesus. It was not yet time to see him. Instead, they told Jesus everything that had happened over the past few days. They confessed their loss of hope and their skepticism about the rumors swirling around Jerusalem.

Their fellow traveler, Jesus, rebuked the sluggishness of their hearts to believe what the prophets had said about how the Messiah would first suffer and then enter his glory (Lk. 24:25-26). Jesus ministered the Word to them as he explained the Scriptures which spoke of him. The Word interpreted the events of the last three days—the cross and the resurrection are the suffering and glory of the Messiah.

As the three neared Emmaus, the two disciples urged him to lodge with them that evening and to enjoy their hospitality. The disciples would host Jesus for that evening, but their guest became the host. As they sat down at the table, Jesus assumed the role of host. This is only the third meal in Luke where Jesus functions as the host. The other two are the feeding of the five thousand (Luke 9) and the Last Supper (Lk. 22). No doubt it surprised the two disciples when Jesus took the bread and began to act as the host of the table.

Jesus' actions exactly parallel the Last Supper. At the table, Jesus "took bread, blessed and broke it, and gave it to them" (Lk. 24:30). This is the language of the Last Supper where Jesus took the bread, gave thanks, broke and gave it (Lk. 22:19). In Luke 22 Jesus said he would eat with his disciples again and then in Luke 24 he does. The narrative clues are abundant: he said he would and he did, Luke uses the same language to describe the breaking of the bread, Jesus is the host and the meaning of the meal is the life of Jesus. Narratively, Luke identifies this meal with the Last Supper. This breaking of the bread is the first "Lord's supper." As a guest in the home of another, he assumes the role of host and makes this meal his. In so doing he reveals himself to his disciples.

In the breaking of the bread, Jesus was "made known" to the disciples (Lk. 24:35). They now "recognized" him when they previously did not because their eyes were opened at the table (Lk. 24:16, 31). The significance of this moment was not lost on the two disciples. They had seen the risen Lord and returned to Jerusalem to tell the other disciples who were now also convinced that Jesus was alive. Then Jesus appeared to the whole group and ate with them (Lk. 24:34-42) and ministered the Word to all of them as he explained the Scriptures regarding his suffering and resurrection (Lk. 24:44-49).

The table is a table of hope as it declares the presence of the kingdom through the resurrection of Jesus. The table proclaims the living Christ. The living host is present at the table eating and drinking with his disciples. The table is about hope, joy and thanksgiving. The table on that first Easter, on that first Sunday, was a table of joy and celebration. There was no solemnity, sadness or burdened hearts. Their response was worship and joy (Lk. 24:52).

Luke 24, as a narrative model of the Lord's supper, should inform the practice of the contemporary church. The first experience of the disciples with the resurrected Christ at a table should shape the practice and experience of the church as it sits at table with Jesus. As LaVerediere comments,

> The story also showed how the Eucharist, while referring to the past, is an event of the present. The Eucharist is not only the memorial of the passion-resurrection of Christ. It is the Lord's supper. The risen Lord, living gloriously in the kingdom, is present at the Table of the Lord. However, in order to recognize him, to really know him, we must be open to his word, making sense of the passion of our lives.[2]

For example, the Word and table are the focal point of the story, and they should be the focal points of Christian assemblies of worship. The Word must interpret the table as it embodies the Word. The table without the Word is subject to misunderstanding and vacuous. But the Word without the table misses the experience of the living Christ as host. The two belong together.

Further, just as the narrative moves from the non-recognition of Jesus to the recognition of Jesus at the table, so the church recognizes Jesus at the table. Jesus is revealed in the context of table. The table is the living presence of Christ. It is a moment when God's presence in Jesus is experienced and made known. At the table we recognize the victory of the resurrection as we eat and drink in hope. At the table we leave all our "Fridays" behind us and celebrate the victory of Christ on Sunday. The table transforms "Friday" into "Sunday." Unfortunately, the church still generally practices the supper as if it were still Friday rather than Sunday. But through the supper we celebrate Sunday and God's victory over Friday. Sunday reinterprets and renews our Fridays. The church should no longer eat on Sunday as if it were Friday.

But the narrative is also a story about welcoming a stranger to the table and a commission to the disciples to bear witness to gospel among all nations (Lk. 24:45-49). Just as the disciples offered hospitality to a stranger on the way, so the table is a place where the church welcomes strangers (aliens). This implies that the table has a missionary quality as well, especially in light of the fact that the disciples receive their call to missions at a table. LaVerdiere comments,

> The Eucharist is an event in which we welcome the stranger to our community. It is an event from which we are sent out on mission. The story of Emmaus showed the Lord revealing himself in the experience of Eucharist. The next story shows the Lord, present at Eucharist, sending the community to all nations. If the church is community by its very nature, it is also missionary by its very nature.[3]

Breaking Bread in Jerusalem

Forty-nine days later the disciples waiting in Jerusalem are "clothed with power from on high" as Jesus had promised (Lk.

24:49; Acts 2:1-4). Jesus poured out the Spirit on his disciples (Acts 2:33) and gave public witness to his Lordship and Messianic status (Acts 2:36). In response, three thousand people were immersed that Sunday (Acts 2:41) and they formed a new community of people as they joined the 120 disciples who had been waiting for the coming Spirit (cf. Acts 1:15).

This new community of Jesus' disciples is described in Acts 2:42 as those who "devoted themselves to the apostles' teaching and fellowship, to the breaking of bread and to prayers." The exact point of Acts 2:42's structure is ambiguous. Luke may be describing four different activities: (1) teaching; (2) fellowship; (3) breaking of bread; and (4) prayers. However, he is probably describing two main activities, (1) teaching and (2) fellowship, and then fellowship is subdivided as (a) breaking bread and (b) prayers.

In other words, Acts 2:42 may describe two ways in which this new community expressed fellowship, that is, they communed through breaking of bread and prayers. This is indicated by the use of "and" (*kai*) in Acts 2:42. Teaching and fellowship are conjoined by the first "and." Breaking of bread and prayers are conjoined by a second "and." The second group stand in appositional relation to the last word of the first group, that is, "breaking of bread and prayers" explain the meaning of "fellowship."

If this understanding is correct, Luke directly links the "breaking of bread" with fellowship (*koinonia*). The breaking of bread is communion. It is a shared experience within the community. It is a shared meal. But this is not all that the disciples shared in Jerusalem. They also shared their possessions. Luke writes that they "had all things in common" (*koina*). The early disciples experienced *koinonia* (fellowship) through shared meals and shared wealth. The fellowship of the disciples was concrete and visible rather than just "spiritual" and invisible. The love of the disciples meant that they shared their lives, including food and material possessions (cf. 1 John 3:17).

Luke wants his readers to link the "breaking of bread" with the previous events in his Gospel. Three times in his Gospel Luke gives a full description of Jesus' actions as host when he took the bread, blessed it, broke it and gave it to his disciples. When he summarily and cryptically refers to the "breaking of bread" in Acts, he assumes the reader knows the fuller stories of his Gospel. Indeed, he assumes they understand the theological significance of "breaking bread." That significance is indicated by Luke 24:35 as the "hinge" text in the "breaking of bread" stories. As the chart below visually represents, when the disciples of Christ broke bread they experienced the presence of the living Christ.

The early church, as a community, celebrated the presence

The Gospel of Luke	Hinge Text	The Book of Acts
Luke 9:16 Jesus took bread, blessed, broke and gave it.		Acts 2:42 the disciples continued in the breaking of bread
Luke 22:19 Jesus took bread, gave thanks, broke and gave it.	Luke 24:35 Jesus was "made known to them in the breaking of the bread"	Acts 2:46 the disciples broke bread daily in their homes
Luke 24:30 Jesus took bread, blessed, broke and gave it.		Acts 20:7 the disciples gathered to break bread

of Christ through the breaking of bread (cf. Paul's use of "breaking bread" in 1 Cor. 10:16). In the light of Luke's Gospel, the breaking of bread refers to a meal with Jesus. It is a meal where the living presence is revealed. When the disciples "broke bread" they experienced the presence of Christ at the table as host.

Acts 2:41-47 is a paradigmatic picture of the new covenant community. It models the Christian community and provides a reference point for the development of Christian life and practice throughout the whole of Acts. In particular, Acts 2:42 functions paradigmatically for the rest of chapter two. The disciples "devoted themselves to the apostles' teaching" because of the "wonders and signs" they performed (Acts 2:43). The disciples also devoted themselves to "fellowship" and they expressed this through sharing their possessions with the needy (Acts 2:44-45). In summary fashion, Luke concretizes Acts 2:42 by describing the daily experience of the Jerusalem church in Acts 2:46-47.

Day by day, as they spent much time together in the temple, they broke bread at home and ate their food with glad and generous hearts, praising God and having the good will of all the people. And day by day the Lord added to their number those who were being saved.

This new community gathered daily in the temple and in homes. Presumably, given the activities in the rest of Acts, they gathered in the temple for prayers and the teaching of the apostles. In Acts 3:1 Peter and John went up to the temple at the time of prayer. The apostles taught and prayed in the temple (Acts 3:1; 5:21), and this was a daily activity (Acts 5:42). Consequently, the daily presence of the disciples at the temple was for prayer and teaching.

But this new community also gathered daily in homes for the fellowship of breaking bread. They shared food with joy and generosity. There is no reason to distinguish between the breaking of bread in Acts 2:42 and Acts 2:46—they refer to a meal in the context of which the liturgical pattern was displayed [breaking bread], the Lord was remembered, and his presence celebrated. The structural connectedness of Acts 2:41-47 means that 2:42 and 2:46 refer to the same kind of "breaking bread."

Whatever this "breaking bread" is ought to be interpreted against the background of Luke 22 and 24 so that those texts inform our understanding of Acts 2. It is incredulous that Luke would use the same language ("breaking bread") to describe two different things within the space of five verses, especially when the Gospel of Luke informs our understanding of what it means to break bread. Consequently, "breaking bread" in Acts 2:42 and 2:46 refer to the Lord's supper which was experienced as a daily meal in the Jerusalem church.

Due to its paradigmatic nature, Acts 2:42-47 should inform the contemporary experience of the Lord's supper in the church. Clearly, since "food" was eaten at this supper, the Lord's supper was a meal. Indeed, it served the function of *koinonia* in a concrete way. The disciples not only shared their material possessions with those in need, but they shared their food as well. The Lord's supper had a social function. In this way, the church shared food with the poor in their community. As Yoder comments, "What the New Testament is talking about wherever the theme is 'breaking bread' is that people actually were sharing with one another their ordinary day-to-day material sustenance."[4] This is the economic meaning of the supper and to "do rightly the practice of breaking bread together is a matter of economic ethics."[5]

This economic dimension of sharing food with the needy explains the "daily" dimension of "breaking bread." It is part of what the community held in "common" (Acts 2:44; 4:32) so that there were no needy persons among them (Acts 4:34). This was part of the "daily" life of the church, as the ministry to the widows illustrates as well (Acts 6:1). "Breaking bread" was central to this daily experience as disciples gathered to commune with each other by sharing food in the presence of the living Christ. If the Lord's supper is understood as a meal, then its "daily" character is understandable as people must eat every day. The Lord's supper, then, was not a mere corporate worship ritual, but the daily experience of worship (praising God) in a community of disciples who ate their "common" food together.

This experience is characterized by joy rather than sadness. It was interactive, celebrative and communal. Unfortunately the current practice of the churches of God does not mirror the kind of excitement which the Jerusalem church experienced.

Breaking Bread in Troas

In Acts 20, Paul is journeying back to Jerusalem with a collection of money for the poor saints. As Luke records this travelogue he includes the story of breaking bread in Troas (Acts 20:7-12).

> On the first day of the week, when we met to break bread, Paul was holding a discussion with them; since he intended to leave the next day, he continued speaking until midnight. There were many lamps in the room upstairs where we were meeting. A young man named Eutychus, who was sitting in the window, began to sink off into a deep sleep while Paul talked still longer. Overcome by sleep, he feel to the ground three floors below and was picked up dead. But Paul went down, and bending over him took him in his arms, and said, "Do not be alarmed, for his life is in him." Then Paul went upstairs, and after he had broken bread and eaten, he continued to converse with them until dawn; then he left. Meanwhile they had taken the boy away alive and were not a little comforted.

The intentional character of "breaking bread" is obvious. The church gathered in order to break bread. This was its explicit purpose for assembling. Paul's sermon was an addendum or special circumstance. But Luke does not tell this story simply to note another Pauline sermon or to describe a Christian assembly. Rather, Luke tells this story because it combines several elements which illuminate the connection between breaking bread, the first day of the week and resurrection. Luke tells this story because on this particular first day of the week when the disciples were gathered to break bread the church experienced firsthand a resurrection from the dead.

The combination of these factors connects this story with Luke 24 which should inform our reading of Acts 20. The parallels between Acts 20 and Luke 24 (reflected in the chart below) indicate that Luke wants us to read Acts 20 in the light of Luke 24, and then also in the light of Luke 22. Both Acts 20 and Luke 24 record the combination of three significant and complementary ideas: breaking bread, first day of the week and resurrection.

Topic	Luke 24	Acts 20
Gathering of Disciples	24:33	20:7
Breaking of Bread	24:30,35	20:7,11
Eating Together	24:42-43	20:11
First Day of the Week	24:1,13	20:7
Teaching the Word (*logos*)	24:44	20:7
Conversation (*omileo*)	24:14-15	20:11
A Rising from the Dead	24:5,46	20:10,12
Fear	24:37-38	20:11
The Living One (*zota*)	24:5	20:12

The Greek text of Acts 20:7, though some translations read "Saturday evening," clearly identifies the day of meeting as the "first day of the week." While sabbath after sabbath Paul had been in the synagogues speaking to Jews (cf. Acts 13:14, 44; 17:2; 18:4), when he encounters a Christian group, they are meeting on the first day of the week. It is uncertain whether this assumes a Jewish reckoning of time (sunset to sunset, so that Acts 20 = Saturday evening) or a Roman reckoning (sunrise to sunrise, so that Acts 20 = Sunday evening). Given the

Gentile character of Troas, it was probably a Sunday evening.[6] Either way, they met on the first day of the week rather than on the sabbath and this is in stark contrast with synagogue meetings in Acts.

The "first day of the week" connects this text theologically with Luke 24. This is no mere temporal indicator or incidental reference. Rather, seen in the light of Luke 24, it is a theological marker. There is theological significance to the "first day of the week" as the day of resurrection and the birthday of the church (Pentecost; cf. Lev. 23:15-21, 33-36). The first day of the week is rooted in the saving act of God in the gospel. The day has redemptive-historical significance as its explicit notation in each of the Gospel stories stresses (Matt. 28:1; Mk. 16:1-2; Lk. 24:1; John 20:1).[7] Jesus as the "first fruit" (1 Corinthians 15:20-23) was raised seven weeks before Pentecost just as the first fruits of the harvest were offered to God before the rest of the harvest was gathered and celebrated at Pentecost (Lev. 23:9-14). The Spirit was poured out and the new community inaugurated on the first day of the week in celebration of the "first fruit" seven weeks prior.

On the first day of the week, Jesus first appeared to his disciples, broke bread with them and ate in their presence (Lk. 24:13, 30, 33, 46), and one week later did the same thing (John 20:19, 26). The first day of the week, then, as resurrection day and as the day that Jesus ate with his disciples became designated as the day when disciples would gather weekly to break bread together. While the Jerusalem church did this daily, daily observances were not uniform throughout the whole church as Troas appears to have turned the daily observance into a weekly one. The weekly observance became standard in the late first and mid-second centuries as indicated by the *Didache* (14:1) and Justin Martyr (*First Apology*, 46-47). However, Ignatius (died ca. 115) exhorted the Ephesians to celebrate the Eucharist "more frequently" (*Ephesians* 13:1), which presumably means more than just Sunday. By the time of Cyprian of Carthage (ca. 253) there were daily celebrations of the Eucharist (*Letters* 57.3). Luke's language, in fact, may reflect a common way of expressing the Sunday gathering since the language of "gathering," "breaking bread," and "first day of the week" are commonly linked in early literature (cf. 1 Cor. 11:20; 16:1; *Didache* 14:1; Ignatius, *Ephesians* 20:2).

Consequently, "first day of the week" is no incidental reference. On the contrary, it reflects the intentional linkage of Acts 20 with Luke 24 in the light of the resurrection story that Acts 20 describes. Both Luke 24 and Acts 20 describe a situation of death which gives birth to life. Jesus emerges from the tomb "alive" and Eutychus goes home "alive," though they were both dead. The resurrection of Eutychus is a concrete experience of victory for the church at Troas. When they gathered to break bread with the risen Eutyches, they ate with a visible example of the kind of hope they celebrated in the light of the resurrection of Jesus. That supper was a celebration of hope and life as we imagine the Troas assembly sitting across the table from Eutychus as they broke bread together. The congregation was greatly "comforted," which is what the contemporary church should experience as it breaks bread together in the presence of the living Christ.

Unfortunately, some read this text as if there were two different breakings of bread. But the text does not say that they broke the bread in Acts 20:7, but only that they came together to break bread. They did not break the bread until after Paul's homily and Eutychus' resurrection. When they return to the third floor, then they broke bread and ate. The unity of breaking bread and eating is the same as Acts 2:46, and describes the meal which characterized the Lord's supper. Breaking bread is a meal where the disciples eat together in the presence of the living Christ and, in this case, in the presence of the resurrected Eutychus.

The coordination of the first day of the week, breaking bread and resurrection gives theological substance to the weekly celebration of the Lord's supper as it bears witness to the living presence of Christ within the community. Given that early Christians met every first day of the week (1 Cor. 16:1), and that they gathered to eat the Lord's supper (1 Cor. 11:20; Acts 20:7), there are good historical reasons for believing that Christians met every first day of the week in order to eat the Lord's supper. More importantly, there are theological reasons for affirming this due to the intersection of the first day of the week, resurrection and breaking bread. The first day of the week is the day of remembrance, the day of our deliverance, because it is the day on which God raised Jesus from the dead and created his new community, the church. The same reason the church gathers every first day of the week is the same reason it should eat the Lord's supper every first day of the week.

Whatever reason one might offer for not eating every Sunday, the same reason could be given for not meeting. Whatever reason one might offer for meeting every Sunday, the same reason could be given for eating. It is a day of worship and a day of celebration because of what God has done in the gospel, and the gospel is proclaimed in the Lord's supper. If the Lord's supper is a celebration of the resurrection, why omit the very ordinance God has given us to celebrate it when we gather on the first day of the week to celebrate the resurrection? If gathering every first day of the week to celebrate our redemption through the gospel is appropriate, why is not the use of God's gift of the Lord's supper equally appropriate? The church as a whole should return to the early Christian practice of breaking bread every Sunday.

Conclusion

"Breaking bread" in Luke-Acts is a covenant meal where the Lord is present as host and we sit together as a community of his disciples in the hope of the resurrection. We share our food with each other as an expression of the communion that exists among the disciples by virtue of God's redemptive act in Jesus. As we eat, we anticipate the eschatological kingdom in which all disciples will share. We will all sit at the Lord's table in his kingdom.

"Breaking bread," then, was not a solemn funeral but a celebration by the new community in which God has revealed the eschaton (resurrection) on the basis of the expiatory sacrifice of the body and blood of Christ. The disciples ate with joy and generosity as they praised God for his redemptive work. They ate with hope as they re-experienced the victory of Jesus over death through eating together. Indeed, these celebratory meals were filled with joyous interaction and enthusiastic outbursts of praise. The word which describes the joy of breaking bread in Acts 2:46 may be literally translated "resounding jubilation" or "enthusiastic outbursts."[8] Joy is pervasive in Luke's meal stories and is analogous to the joy that characterized the sacrificial meals of the Old Testament (Deut. 12:7, 12, 18; 14:26; 27:7). It is one of the great discontinuities between the meals in Luke and the contemporary church that joy is not the major way in which the contemporary supper is experienced.

Questions for Discussion

1. What is the theological meaning of the Lord's supper according to the story of "breaking bread" in Luke 24?

2. How should the resurrection function in our understanding of the meaning of the Lord's supper? Is this meaning under-emphasized in the contemporary practice of the supper? Why?

3. What is the theological point of Acts 20:7-12? What is the relationship between the first day of the week, the resurrection and the supper?

4. What is atmosphere of "breaking bread" in Luke-Acts? Is it joy or solemnity? How should this affect our understanding of the supper in the contemporary church?

PART III.

COMMUNION IN PAUL:
EATING WITH EACH OTHER

7 / COVENANT RENEWAL
IN 1 CORINTHIANS 10

The problems in Corinth were multiple, but interrelated. Various kinds of factions divided the church, including allegiances to different teachers (1 Cor. 1:12) and different socio-economic strata (1 Cor. 4:8; 11:21-22). Sexual immorality was pervasive, including incest (1 Cor. 5:1) and prostitution (1 Cor. 6:15-16). Spiritual arrogance dominated the church as they exalted knowledge over love (1 Cor. 8:1-3) and asserted the superiority of their own spiritual status or gifts (1 Cor. 13:1-3). Their "spiritual" sense distorted their understanding of marriage (1 Cor. 7:1-7), denied the future bodily resurrection of the saints (1 Cor. 15:12) and enabled them to eat in pagan sanctuaries at idolatrous tables (1 Cor. 10:18-22).

These problems are fundamentally interrelated. Some believe the root problem is a kind of overrealized eschatology where the Corinthians believed that they had already "arrived" spiritually, that is, they fully participated in the life of the Spirit.[1] Consequently, they already had spiritual bodies (thus no need for a future resurrection) and this excused sexual immorality (the body has no spiritual value). Others believe the root problem is the pagan environment and background of the Corinthians.[2] The Corinthian church was primarily pagan in origin (cf. 1 Cor. 12:2) and those pagan values still shaped their ethical and spiritual perspectives.

"The mores, patterns of culture and specific religious institutions of Greco-Roman paganism," Oster writes, "must be seen as the soil in which the Corinthian problems were germinated and grew."[3] Paganistic syncretism generated the problems in Corinth. It fostered arrogance in Hellenistic wisdom, exalted knowledge, devalued the body and marriage, denied the resurrection and promoted Greco-Roman socio-economic distinctions in the church. Their pagan heritage encouraged sexual immorality and participation at idolatrous festivals.

At bottom, paganism connects all the problems at Corinth. Shaped by their pagan heritage, culture and religiosity, the Corinthians distorted Christian ethics and practice. In particular, the Lord's supper was distorted by those pagan values. In two places in 1 Corinthians (10:14-22 and 11:17-34), Paul addresses how pagan culture had reshaped the Lord's supper in such a way that it was no longer the Lord's supper, but their own. Culture compromised the Lord's table with pagan ethical and social values and transformed the table of the Lord into something foreign and indemincal to the gospel. When culture invaded the church at Corinth, it distorted the gospel when it distorted the Lord's table.

Paul comments on the Lord's supper first in 1 Corinthians 10. The wider context of 1 Corinthians 10 is chapters 8-10 and the subject is Christian freedom. In particular, the overarching question for the freedom of the Christian is whether to eat food that had been sacrificed to idols (1 Cor. 8:9). This was a complicated question because the meat was sometimes eaten as part of an idolatrous feast in the pagan temple, at other times sold in the marketplace and at still other times shared as part of hospitality in a pagan and/or Christian home (1 Cor. 10:23-30). The answer to such a complicated contextual problem in Corinthian culture was not simple.

Paul's basic solution is to choose love over knowledge, that is, to relinquish the right to eat such meat for the sake of the conscience of the other (1 Cor. 8:11-13). Paul affirms that the freedom to love trumps the freedom to eat. Nevertheless, he acknowledges the legitimacy of eating meat that had been sold in the marketplace as well as eating in the homes of others as a function of receiving hospitality. Paul does not condemn those who eat food sacrificed to idols, but cautions that they must eat in good conscience and with appropriate deference to the weak.

However, Paul does condemn one form of eating. Apparently, some Corinthians, who knew there was only one God and therefore that idols were nothing (cf. 1 Cor. 8:4), did not hesitate to participate in idolatrous meals at pagan temples. They would sit at the Lord's table on Sunday and then sit at the table of idols at other times. In their arrogant knowledge, they sat at two tables and served two masters. In 1 Corinthians 10:1-22 Paul addresses the arrogant who had grown conceited by their knowledge. Paul uses the covenantal character of the Lord's supper to counter the problem of arrogant idolatry among the Corinthians. The "spiritual" of Corinth apparently thought themselves inviolate because of their participation in the spiritual reality of Christ.

The Example of Israel

To counter this spiritual arrogance Paul rehearses the history of the Exodus and the wilderness. He describes both their spiritual privilege as redeemed people (1 Cor. 10:1-4) and their moral failure as rebellious sinners (1 Cor. 10:5-10).

Paul's language stresses the identity between Israel and the Corinthian church. Though Gentiles, they are the descendants of Israel. They share identity with ancient Israel as the people of God. Further, Paul uses the language of the New Testament "sacraments" to describe the redemption of Israel. Israel, as were the Corinthians, was "baptized" and "ate" and "drank." Israel was baptized "into Moses in the cloud and in the sea" just as the Corinthians were baptized "into the name of Christ" (1 Cor. 1:13) in the Spirit (1 Cor. 6:11; 12:13) and in the water. Israel was a baptized people, just as the Corinthians were.

Further, Israel "ate the same spiritual food" and "drank the same spiritual drink" as the Corinthians. Israel ate manna in the wilderness and drank water from the rock in the wilderness. The identity between Israel and Corinth is not simply that they both eat and drink, but that they eat and drink the same spiritual reality, which is Christ. What the Corinthians eat and drink in the Lord's supper was shared by Israel in the wilderness.

This baptismal and eucharistic typological language stresses the identity between Israel and Corinth. Both experienced God's redemption. Both experienced God's spiritual nourishment. Both experienced Christ. "Nevertheless," Paul writes, "God was not pleased with most of them (Israelites), and they were struck down in the wilderness" (1 Cor. 10:5). Their "spiritual" status did not insulate them from God's wrath or excuse them from covenantal obedience. On the contrary, their spiritual privilege should have fostered obedience.

Just as Paul identified the shared spiritual reality between Israel and Corinth, so he also rehearses the history of Israel to point out their shared moral failure. The specifics of Israel's moral failure are exactly the problems that have appeared in the Corinthian church. Israel, therefore, constitutes an "example" (or type, *tupoi*) for the Corinthians from which they should learn (1 Cor. 10:6). Their lot will be the same as Israel if they continue to pursue an unethical lifestyle.

The sins of Israel are listed in 1 Corinthians 10:6-10. Israel became an idolatrous nation and indulged in "sexual immorality." Further, they tested the Lord with their disobedience and complained about God's faithlessness to his promises. Corinth was also endangered by idolatry and sexual immorality, and the presumption of spiritual arrogance tested the Lord. Israel's history reminds Corinth that even though they had eaten and drunk from the same spiritual resource—Christ, it did not guarantee their covenantal relationship regardless of lifestyle. Many in Israel died and were destroyed. Corinthian believers were now in a similar circumstance. Their arrogance had blinded them to the danger of falling (1 Cor. 10:12).

The fundamental point, of course, is to alert the Corinthians to the reality of covenantal obligation. "Sacramental" experiences—baptism and the Lord's supper—do not guarantee redemption. Salvation is experienced through baptism and the Lord's supper, but these ordinances involve believers in covenantal commitments. They call believers to an ethical lifestyle that imitates the Lord. Worship without ethics has always been unacceptable (e.g., Jeremiah 7), and no baptism or table can save those who arrogantly violate their covenantal commitments.

Lord's Supper as Communion

The key term in 1 Corinthians 10:14-22 is "communion" (*koinonia/koinonous*; variously translated "sharing" or "participation"). Further, the term "partake" (*metechomen/metechein*) in the following quotation, which shares the same thought-world as "communion," is also highlighted in italics below.

> Therefore, my dear friends, flee from the worship of idols. I speak as to sensible people; judge for yourselves what I say. The cup of blessing that we bless, is it not a *sharing* in the blood of Christ? The bread that we break, is it not a *sharing* in the body of Christ? Because there is one bread, we who are many are one body, for we all *partake* of one bread. Consider the people of Israel; are not those who eat the sacrifices *partners* in the altar? What do I imply then? That food sacrificed to idols is anything, or that an idol is anything? No, I imply that

what pagans sacrifice, they sacrifice to demons and not
to God. I do not want you to be *partners* with demons.
You cannot drink the cup of the Lord and the cup of
demons. You cannot *partake* of the Table of the Lord
and the table of demons. Or are we provoking the Lord
to jealousy? Are we stronger than he?

Eating and drinking entails "communion" (or fellowship).
When Israel ate their sacrifices, they fellowshipped the altar.
When pagans ate their sacrifices, they fellowshipped demons.
When Christians eat and drink, they fellowship the body and
blood of Christ. To understand this "fellowship" is to appreciate why one cannot both "partake" of the Lord's table and the
table of demons.

There are two levels to this "communion." First, there is
communion with the body and blood of Christ. Historically, this
idea has been debated interminably. "Is it not a sharing in the
blood of Christ" is just as subject to various interpretations as
"this is my blood." The problem is the meaning of "is." This is
complicated by the association of the verb with the term
koinonia (fellowship). For some this means that Christians physically (substantially) eat and drink the body and blood of Christ.
For others it means that the bread and wine symbolically represent the body and blood of Christ. For still others a genuine spiritual reality is experienced through eating and drinking.

As indicated in my discussion of the words of institution in
Luke 22 (chapter 5), this debate is rather misguided. Though
there is a mysterious connection between the altar and the table
so that the reality of Christ's work is experienced through eating and drinking, it is best to take our cue from Paul's own
explanatory words. He points his readers to the sacrifices of
Israel. When they ate the sacrifices they participated in (fellowshipped) the altar. Israel's sacrifices, as discussed in chapter three, were eaten in the presence of God. God sat at table

with Israel and shared his *shalom* with his people. The meal was a moment of fellowship between God and his people. To fellowship the altar is to fellowship God through the atoning significance of the altar.

To eat and drink at the Lord's table in his kingdom is to eat and drink with Christ. We fellowship Christ and experience the reality of spiritual communion through the altar of Christ's body and blood. The spiritual communion of the table is the spiritual presence of Christ at the table. We embrace the altar's atoning significance (the body and blood of Christ) as we eat with Jesus at the table. To fellowship the altar, then, is to enjoy and experience the atoning benefits of the altar. Just as the altar enabled Israel to sit at table with God, so the cross enables Christians to sit at table with Jesus. Thus, eating and drinking at the table of the Lord means to experience the *shalom* which the altar produced between God and his people.

However, communion with Christ involves covenantal responsibility. Since whoever eats the sacrifice participates in the altar, to eat the sacrifice is a matter of covenantal commitment. One cannot eat at the table of the Lord and at the table of demons (idolatry). To do both would provoke the covenant Lord to jealousy for his covenant people (1 Cor. 10:21-22). To eat from the Lord's table means to be committed to the Lord's covenant. To drink the Lord's cup is to renew our covenant with God through Christ. Just as the fellowship offering appeared again and again at key redemptive moments as covenant renewal, so every Lord's day is a covenant renewal for God's people through the Lord's supper.

A second level of meaning is communion with the body of Christ, the church. Paul emphasizes the oneness of the church at the table. Though many, the church is one because it shares the one bread at the table. The unity of the church is rooted in the "common union"[4] the church shares in Christ who has made the church one. When the church eats and drinks it shares the same body and blood. By visibly eating and drinking together the church exhibits the unity of the body in Christ. When we sit at the same table, we testify to our shared experienced of the shared reality of Jesus Christ.

The communion of the altar in the new covenant meal is a communion of many members as one body. The covenant meal means to share in the blessings of God's work in Christ, and the meal means that we come before him as the one covenant people of God. Our communion is a participation in the one spiritual reality which was created by the offering of the body and blood of Christ. As the body of Christ, the church, we share that reality with each other. Though there are many members, there is one body of fellowship which is focused on Christ's work rather than the ministry of its diverse members (cf. 1 Cor. 1:13; 3:5, 21-23). The covenant meal is a communal meal where the people of God are united to each other by their covenant with the one God.

Thus, the covenant meal at the table of the Lord is a "meal shared *between believers* and *with their Lord*."[5] This means that similar meals with believers in other gods and with their idols is excluded. Believers cannot sit at both tables. They can only serve one Lord and they can only share the life of one community. Christians have a singular commitment to the Lordship of Jesus and, consequently, they may only sit at one table.

The connection between idolatry and jealousy is a strong Old Testament theme (Ps. 78:58; Deut. 4:24; 32:21; Ex. 20:5; 34:14; Josh. 24:19). The dual commitment with which idolaters partake of the Lord's supper draws the anger of God. This points to the seriousness with which the supper must be taken. It is a moment of covenant renewal which entails serious ethical obligation.

The Ethical Meaning of the Supper

The supper is a communal event—the communion of God, the worshipper, and the church in a single experience. The supper, as table, is a communal experience where God, worshipper and church mutually commune. It exhibits reciprocity as God communes with us and we with God and with each other. This is a dynamic spiritual reality in which we all participate. It is mutual witness.

As such, the supper is a divine witness to us. God declares his allegiance to us in Jesus Christ. The gift of the body and blood for our sins enables the gift of his communion. We commune because God has acted for us in Christ. God testifies to his love at the table through the bread and wine. He assures those who eat that he is graciously present and that he is jealous for them. God is committed to his people.

The supper is also our witness to God. It is our vow of commitment. To eat and drink at the Lord's table is to pledge our allegiance to God and enter into his communion. We offer ourselves as gifts at the table as we demonstrate our loyalty by sharing his table. This loyalty extends to the communal level because when we eat, we eat as a body, a community. As one body, we eat the one bread in communion with the one God. This is the language of covenant renewal. The Lord's supper is a moment of rededication and recommitment to the covenant, both by God and ourselves. By communing with us through the body and blood of Christ, God renews his covenant with us. By eating and drinking, we renew our covenant with God and with each other. The Lord's table, then, is a meal where we bind ourselves to the covenant once again.

Consequently, there can be no dual commitments at this table. No one can sit at the table of the Lord and the table of demons at the same time and in the same week. Whoever eats and drinks at the Lord's table commits to the Lordship of Jesus and affirms that they will keep the covenant. Eating a covenant meal entailed the promise to keep the covenant and this promise was made under the threat of death. Whoever failed to keep the covenant experienced the death of the animal sacrificed for the meal. When Christians eat at the Lord's table, they commit to keep the covenant or else experience death.

Israel entered into covenant with God, but they violated it in the wilderness through idolatry and sexual immorality. They died in the wilderness. Their history serves as an example to us. In baptism we enter into covenant with God, and through the supper we renew that covenant weekly. But this renewal obligates us to keep the covenant and live worthy of the gospel (cf. Phil. 1:27). Baptism and the Lord's supper do not guarantee redemption, but they call us to a gospel lifestyle. Ethics is a necessary dimension of the Christian life and the table obligates us.

Whenever we eat and drink, we must ask at whose table do we sit? If we sit at the Lord's table, then we follow that Lord as we participate in his redemptive presence. But if we sit at the Lord's table, we cannot sit at another. The table of the Lord is a singular commitment and admits no other lordship in our lives. To eat and drink at the table of the Lord is to confess that we are disciples of Jesus and follow no one else.

Conclusion

The table is a genuine experience of communion. It is no mere symbolic event. The bread and wine do not simply represent Christ. They mediate the spiritual reality of redemption and salvation. They are a participation in the saving work of Jesus. We eat "spiritual food" and drink "spiritual drink."

However, this is not an occasion for spiritual arrogance. Participation in the spiritual reality of Jesus does not excuse an unethical lifestyle. On the contrary, the invitation to the table of the Lord entails an obligation to honor the Lord of the table. As God's invited guests to the table, we honor the one who shares his table with us. We honor him by sharing his values and imitating his character. We honor him by keeping our covenant just as he keeps his.

The Lord is a jealous God, and his jealousy means that he protects his table. He will not sit at table with the rebellious; he will exclude them just as he expects his people to exclude those who arrogantly pursue sin (1 Cor. 5:11-13). God invites us to his table to experience his communion and he expects those who sit at his table to honor him and accept his Lordship.

Questions for Discussion

1.What is the relationship between ethics and the Lord's supper?

2. What in our contemporary culture would be analogous with eating an idolatrous feast in a pagan temple? How are people often "double minded" in their eating and drinking at the Lord's table?

3. What is meant when we describe the Lord's supper as a "communion"? How does the phrase "the Lord's table" help shape our understanding of this communion?

4. Is the fellowship between Christ and his people merely symbolic? Are the bread and cup merely symbolic?

8 / COMMUNAL EATING IN 1 CORINTHIANS 11

The most extended discussion of the Lord's supper in the New Testament is found in 1 Corinthians 11:17-34. No other text extrapolates from the Last Supper the meaning of the supper as fully as this one in such a focused manner. However, this text is not an elaborate, systematic assessment of the Lord's supper. It is not a piece of systematic theology. On the contrary, it is a narrow, focused response to a specific problem in the Corinthian church. The problem is occasional, that is, it is specific to the situation in Corinth, but the theology is normative. Paul applies the meaning of the supper to the specific problem encountered in Corinth. While we cannot fully understand the meaning of the supper from this text alone, it does provide a specific insight into the normative meaning of the supper for not only the Corinthians, but for us.

In response to the Corinthian situation, Paul articulates a vision of the table as a communal act which transcends all diversity in the body. Paul rebukes the Corinthians for the form of their supper which distorted its meaning. Their form divided the body rather than uniting it. The table became an occasion for factions and divisions rather than the supreme expression of unity. While the Corinthians intended to observe the Lord's supper, they made it into one of their own meals by following the form and cultural mores of their own Greco-Roman practices. The form of their supper denied the meaning of the Lord's supper.

Form does matter. It is not simply a matter of function. Function cannot exist without form and form must serve the function. Function must have an appropriate form that is faithful to the original intent of the supper. Consequently, Paul seeks to correct the corrupted form in order to restore the proper function of the supper.

The Problem in Corinth (1 Corinthians 11:17-22)

The setting of Corinthian assemblies was a home, not a "church building." According to Romans 16:23, which was written from Corinth, the "whole church" met in the home of Gaius. Whether this was the only house church in Corinth is unknown, but it locates the Corinthian assemblies in homes. No doubt Gaius was a fairly wealthy person whose home was, if similar to other wealthy homes, large enough to accommodate an assembly of 40-60 people. These homes usually included a large banquet room to entertain guests at a meal.

As the Corinthian church met in such an environment, the social mores of the Greco-Roman culture in which it lived invaded the Corinthian assembly. It divided the table and transformed it into an occasion of social stratification between rich and poor. This is precisely where Paul locates the table problem in the Corinthian church:

> Now in the following instructions I do not commend you, because when you come together it is not for the better but for the worse. For, to begin with, when you come together as a church, I hear that there are divisions among you; and to some extent I believe it.

Indeed, there have to be factions among you, for only so will it become clear who among you are genuine. When you come together, it is not really to eat the Lord's supper. For when the time comes to eat, each of you goes ahead with your own supper, and one goes hungry and another becomes drunk. What! Do you not have homes to eat and drink in? Or do you show contempt for the church of God and humiliate those who have nothing? What should I say to you? Should I commend you? In this matter I do not commend you!

Paul encounters division (1 Cor. 11:18, *schismata*) and factions (1 Cor. 11:19, *haireseis*). They are not waiting for the whole church to assemble, but they are proceeding with the "supper" before everyone arrives (1 Cor. 11:21, 33). They had gathered to eat the "Lord's supper" but they instead ate their own "supper" because they were hungry and thirsty (1 Cor. 11:20-21,34). This reflected a socio-economic problem in the church since those who had homes would not wait on those who had nothing (1 Cor. 11:22). According to Paul, this violates the tradition which he received from the Lord and had handed on to the Corinthians (1 Cor. 11:23).

The problem is occasioned by the breakdown of unity in the context of a meal. The church in Corinth ate a *deipnon* (supper, 11:20, 21, 25). This was the regular evening meal in the Greco-Roman world. The two major courses of the banquet were the "supper" proper which was followed by the *sumposion* (symposium) which was a drinking party.[1] In a religious context this would have included a chant to a god(s) as, for example, in Plato's *Symposium* 176A. These "suppers" paralleled the Greek practice of *eranos* which was like a Greek "potluck" dinner. It could take place in homes or at sacrificial meals in Greek temples.[2] Its significance is fundamentally *identification*. The meal testifies to the identify of the people of God. It should reflect the gospel values of a people who have been shaped by the cross of Christ rather than shaped by Greco-Roman social conventions. Consequently, Paul did not forbid the meal. Instead, he regulated it in the light of abuses. Paul wanted them to come together "to eat" (1 Cor. 11:33). But they ought to come together as a church or assembly *(ecclesia;* 1 Cor. 11:18) which unites as the body of Christ (1 Cor. 11:29).

Greco-Roman meals were occasions of social stratification, drunkenness and disorderliness. They were also at the center of most social institutions or social occasions (e.g., funerary banquets, sacrificial banquets, philosophical society meetings, trade guild meetings, religious society meetings). Plutarch's *Table Talk* (ca. 100 A.D.) is an example of the extensive discussion of table etiquette in the ancient world. Rick Oster offers this summary of the problems generally associated with Greco-Roman meals:[3]

a. In practice, ancient meals were very hierarchical in arrangement. The high degree of social and economic stratification (rich/poor; free/slaves) that prevailed in the Graeco-Roman world was imported into arrangements for dinner. Accordingly, the best seats, the best food, the best wine, the best company and the best entertainment were reserved for the affluent, the noble born, the free, and the prestigious. Several pagan philosophers and rhetoricians complain about this practice of bringing social stratification into the meal experience. These writers argue that mealtime and the meal experiences should be communal meals that are not destroyed by societal concerns for "rich and poor" or "free and slave."

b. Ancient mealtimes were often characterized by disruptive speech and argumentative cliques. We have testimony both in the literary and epigraphical record from antiquity that religious guilds and fraternal organizations had to adopt "Rules of Order" to keep a sense of orderliness, especially at their symposia or evening meals.[4]

c. Drunkenness was a regular problem at these Graeco-Roman meals and banquets. Both the quantity and the quality of wine served was so important to ancient men and women that there was often an attendant in charge of this (cf. John 2:8-10). Graeco-Roman authors whose values included moderation in drinking criticized their peers who regularly became intoxicated at these meals.

These same problems emerged during the Corinthian meals. The rich divided themselves from the poor so that they ate and drank separated from the poor. The poor, perhaps slaves or lower class workers, arrived later when the food and drink were gone. The poor, then, went hungry while the rich were well-fed and some of them drunk. Instead of transforming Greco-Roman meals by the values of the gospel, the Lord's supper was transformed into a Greco-Roman meal.

Taking pride in their wealth and social status, some Corinthians did not wait for others to arrive. They proceeded with their meal without the whole church present. By this, Paul sarcastically comments, the Corinthians made distinctions among themselves in order to identify those who had been divinely approved (those who were "genuine"). The Corinthians exhibited their spiritual arrogance by dividing the body into the very socio-economic strata that the gospel intended to obliterate. Consequently, the Corinthians demonstrated not only their pride, but their total lack of appreciation for gospel values. The gospel intends to unite diverse groups, transcend cultural and fallen distinctions, and testify to the "common union" of the body of Christ. The Corinthians drank judgment upon themselves because they denied the gospel by the way in which they conducted what was supposed to be the Lord's supper.

The Tradition (1 Corinthians 11:23-26)

As a corrective to the Corinthian practices, Paul points his readers to the Last Supper. The practice of the Lord's supper must be shaped by Jesus' original intent. The Corinthians must remember that this is the *Lord's* supper, and not their own. Consequently, the practice of the supper must be shaped by the proclamation of the gospel rather than by fallen value systems. The gospel must give meaning to the supper, not Greco-Roman cultural values. To that end, Paul recalls the tradition:

> For I received from the Lord what I also handed on to you, that the Lord Jesus on the night when he was betrayed took a loaf of bread, and when he had given thanks, he broke it and said, "This is my body that is for you. Do this in remembrance of me." In the same way he took the cup also, after supper, saying, "This cup is the new covenant in my blood. Do this, as often as you drink it, in remembrance of me." For as often as you eat this bread and drink the cup, you proclaim the Lord's death until he comes.

Paul cites the tradition that the bread was broken in remembrance of Jesus before the supper and, "after supper," the cup was drunk. The language is essentially the same as Luke's account (cf. chapter five). Paul applies this tradition as a norm or standard for the practice of the Lord's supper in Corinth. The supper must be shaped by cross.

This does not mean that the table becomes an altar. To be shaped by the cross means to permit the values of the gospel, which the cross embodies, to shape the table environment. The table must embody the gospel. The table must reflect gospel values and testify to them. In this sense the table proclaims the

"Lord's death." It proclaims the good news of gospel values. It proclaims how the Lord's death has broken down all social, racial, and gender barriers. It proclaims the unity of the body of Christ at the table of the Lord that was accomplished by the cross of Jesus. Proclaiming the death of Christ is the good news that the gospel redeems all fallen structures, but when the table reintroduces those fallen structures it denies the gospel.

Hence, the norm is the *"Lord's* supper." It is his table, not ours. Therefore, we are to treat each other as fellow-servants, as fellow-members of the body. Just as the gospel is for all, so the supper is for all. The meal ought to proclaim the gospel, but Corinthian actions had undermined the gospel itself by dividing the body by socio-economic factors. The Corinthian table did not reflect the values of Christ.

Here form and function must reflect appropriate theological meaning. Form should serve the function of the supper. The Corinthian form undermined the theological meaning of the supper. The contemporary church, like the Corinthian one, needs to give attention to form. Too often the modern church is focused on the order of the elements, the frequency of the supper and other specifics (e.g., unleavened or leavened bread, wine or grape juice, etc.) when the essence of the modern supper is suspect because it has lost its table (supper or meal) form.

The Application (1 Corinthians 11:27-34)

Having confronted the problem (1 Cor. 11:17-22) and asserted the normative tradition (1 Cor. 11:23-26), Paul offers his corrective:

> Whoever, therefore, eats the bread or drinks the cup of the Lord in an unworthy manner will be answerable for the body and blood of the Lord. Examine yourselves, and only then eat the bread and drink of the cup. For all who eat and drink without discerning the body, eat and drink judgment against themselves. For this reason

many of you are weak and ill, and some have died. But if we judged ourselves, we would not be judged. But when we are judged by the Lord, we are disciplined so that we may not be condemned along with the world.

So then, my brothers and sisters, when you come together to eat, wait for one another. If you are hungry, eat at home, so that when you come together, it will not be for your condemnation. About the other things I will give instructions when I come.

Paul believes they should continue to eat the supper (meal), but wait for everyone so that no one will go hungry. Paul does not discard the meal, but encourages them to eat together. In the context of this communal meal where food is shared, the communion of the body and blood of the Lord through the bread and wine will result in a communion with each other through the oneness of the body (1 Cor. 10:16-17). Paul concludes his corrective with three instructions as a resolution to their specific problems.

Instruction 1: wait till everyone arrives before you eat the supper.

Instruction 2: if you are hungry, eat something at home before you assemble so you can wait for everyone to arrive.

Instruction 3: Paul will settle everything else when he arrives.

Whatever else Paul may mean, he instructs them to eat together. Instead of discarding the meal, he instructs them to wait for each other. If they are so hungry that they cannot wait, then they should eat something at home before they come to the assembly. The solution is simple: wait and if you cannot, then eat something at home to hold you over till everyone arrives. The main point is that the church should eat together as a community rather than be divided by socio-economic realities.

Paul argues the need to wait on the ground that the church must "discern the body" when it eats. This phrase has been the subject of considerable controversy. Some argue that it means to "discern" the body (flesh) of Christ as substance in the bread. As a result, communion is closed to those who do not recognize the substance of the body of Christ in bread for fear that they will drink damnation to themselves. Some argue that it refers to the subjective state of the worshippers as they introspectively discern the seriousness of their act of communion and reflect on the meaning of the death of Christ. Indeed, some believe that one must exclusively think about the cross (its gore and lore) in order to worthily discern the body of Christ. These two perspectives understand the word "body" to refer to the physical body of Jesus which suffered on the cross.

However, there is another, and more preferable, understanding. To "discern the body" means to discern the church as a community. It is a directive regarding the communal meaning of the Lord's supper. To discern the body is to partake of the supper in a way that bears witness to not only the unity of the body of Christ (church) but also to the *koinonia* (fellowship) of that body which transcends all social and economic barriers. Thus, Paul's statement is directly linked to the specific problem in the Corinthian assembly. The problem is not that the Corinthians did not think about the cross, but rather the problem was that they did not embody the cross in a communal way at the table.

Other than the contextual problem Paul is addressing, the best indicator that Paul is talking about the church rather than the physical body of Christ is the way he uses his language. When Paul is thinking about the communion of the elements with body and blood of Christ, he uses both "body and blood" as in 1 Corinthians 10:16 and 11:27. However, in 1 Corinthians

11:29, as in 1 Corinthians 10:17, he only refers to the "body." So, just as in 1 Corinthians 10:16-17, Paul subtly shifts from "body and blood" (the physical substance of Jesus) to "body" (the church). The two are intimately connected because it is the body and blood of Christ that grounds the church as a community (the body of Christ). The "common union" of the church is the body and blood of Christ. Consequently, when the church eats and drinks the body and blood of Christ, it does so as the body of Christ (the church). The altar and the table are connected. The altar grounds and enables the table just as the body and blood of Christ grounds and establishes the church as God's one people. At the table, then, worshippers must discern the unity and community of this body in order to eat and drink worthily.

Consequently, to eat and drink worthily is not about private introspection, but about public action. Paul is not stipulating a kind of meditative silence on the cross of Christ or an introspective assessment of our relative holiness. On the contrary, to eat in an "unworthy manner," in this context, is to eat in a divisive manner like that which existed in Corinth. The church must examine itself about the manner in which the supper is conducted (1 Cor. 11:28). There may be many ways to eat the supper unworthily (e.g., 1 Cor. 10:18-21 where Corinthians ate unworthily because they ate with a dual commitment, serving two masters), but the specific unworthiness in 1 Corinthians 11 is a communal problem, not an individualistic one. The church eats worthily when it eats as a united community embodying the values for which Christ died.

When the church fails to embody those values, then it denies the gospel. When it denies the gospel as it eats, then it condemns itself as it eats and drinks judgment upon itself. The Lord's table is a serious matter. It is not serious because it is quiet time or because it functions as penance. Rather, it is serious because as the Lord's supper it bears witness to the gospel.

Judgment comes to those who deny the gospel. It is not about a momentary lapse of focused attention on the cross. It is about embodying the gospel as a community when the church comes together to eat and drink.

Conclusion

As Greco-Roman culture invaded the Corinthian assembly, the Lord's supper became a moment of socio-economic stratification. Modern culture has invaded the contemporary church so that the Lord's supper has become an occasion for silent, individualistic piety. Just as the Corinthians, through their supper, divided the body of Christ along the lines of rich and poor, so modern culture divides the body by restricting the supper to the recesses of each individual's mind. If the Corinthians used the supper to maintain social distinctions in the culture, modernity has transformed the supper into a private event. Both distort the intent of the supper as a public, unifying, communal meal. Both deny the communal character of the table.

Modern culture, with the backing of a long heritage (see chapter nine), has undermined the intent of the table by replacing the table with an altar. As Paul corrects the Corinthian practice of the table, he still affirms the value of eating and drinking. The table remains. In the modern church, there is no table. Some churches have an altar instead of a table, others have placed the table at the rear of the building, and still others have no visible table (or altar) in their buildings. Not only has the supper been reduced to bread and wine, it has lost almost all connection to the "table" environment.

According to Paul, the table must remain because it embodies the communal experience of the supper. Though the meal is abused, he does not jettison it. Instead, the meal must reflect its intended communal function. The Corinthians must wait for everyone to arrive before eating and they must make no socio-economic (or ethnic, or gender) distinctions at their tables. In the same way, the modern church should restore the meal and consequently restore the communal intention of the table as a real table. If the Corinthians needed to wait for everyone to come to the table for the meal, the modern church needs to restore the table as a meal.

Form is important. The Corinthians distorted the supper by reshaping its form and investing it with values that arose out of their fallen, pagan culture. The modern church dangerously distorts the supper as well. When the form of the supper is reduced to bread and wine, restricted to a formal, ritual context, and stressed as a private moment between the worshipper and God, then the function of the supper is distorted. The contemporary form of the supper is problematic because it fails to fully embody the biblical function of the supper. In this case, "revisioning the supper" means to restore the meal and renew the communal meaning of the table.

Discussion Questions

1. Was the supper in 1 Corinthians a meal? What points in the text disclose the nature of the supper?

2. What was the problem with the conduct of the supper in Corinth? How might this same problem show itself in your congregation? Do you see any analogies?

3. What does it mean to "discern the body"? How does one's answer to this question reflect either an individual or communal focus for the supper?

4. Is the practice of the supper in your congregation more individualistic or communal? Where does the emphasis fall? Where should it fall? How might the supper be conducted to reflect more communal goals?

PART IV.

COMMUNION TODAY:
A CALL FOR SUPPER REFORM
AND RENEWAL

9 / A BRIEF HISTORY OF TABLE AND ALTAR

The previous survey of biblical literature highlighted the importance of table in biblical theology. The table was the meeting place of God and humanity in Israel's sacrificial meals, including the Passover. Jesus ate with both saints and sinners during his ministry, and he ate a Last Supper with his disciples. After the resurrection, Jesus ate with his disciples again and the church broke bread together daily. The Lord's supper in the New Testament was a table of shared food. It was a meal.

However, the contemporary practice of the supper has lost its table environment. The altar has replaced the table. The atmosphere has shifted from celebrative, interactive joy at a table to silent, private meditation at the altar. The contemplative sorrow of the cross has replaced the joy of the resurrection.

The discontinuity between Acts 2:46 and the contemporary observance of the Lord's supper is so obvious that many conclude that Acts 2:46 cannot refer to the supper. But this discontinuity is having the wrong hermeneutical effect. Instead of our present observance of the Lord's supper reinterpreting Acts 2:46, the experience of the Jerusalem church in Acts 2:46 should reshape the contemporary practice of the Lord's supper.

The dissonance between Acts 2:46 and the present is due to the historical shift that reshaped the Eucharistic meal early in the history of the church. It is important to understand the significance of that shift in order to appreciate the present setting of the Eucharistic altar. Understanding the shift will enable a renewed appreciation for the table-orientation of the supper.

The Shift from Table to Altar

The earliest record of the Eucharist outside of the New Testament is found in the *Didache* (also known as the "Teaching of the Twelve Apostles"). The final form of the document was probably published towards the end of the first century (ca. 100 A.D.). At this point, the Eucharist was still a meal. As a church manual, it instructs the readers to "give thanks" at the "Eucharist" in the form of traditional Jewish meal prayers (9:1).[1] It gives thanks for the cup first as the prayer expresses gratitude for "holy vine of David" which has been "made known to us through Jesus" (9:2). It gives thanks for the "broken bread" second as the prayer expresses gratitude for "the life and knowledge" which God "made known to us through Jesus" (9:3). Strikingly absent is any reference to the body and blood of Christ or the traditional words of institution ("this is my body;" "this is my blood"). The meal setting is clearly indicated by the phrase "and after you have had enough" (10:1). The framework fits with ritual Jewish meals (as in Old Testament festivals), but also fits the table ministry of Jesus. "At this point in the community's history," LaVerdiere comments, "the meals were inspired by and held in direct continuity with those Jesus shared with his disciples in the course of his ministry."[2]

Ignatius, martyred around 115 A.D., also hints that the meal was still part of the Eucharistic ritual. At the same time, we see in Ignatius the initial shift from table to altar. Table or altar, the Eucharist is the centerpiece of the Christian assembly and the focal point of Christian unity, according to Ignatius. His seven letters are filled with references to the Lord's supper, some are incidental and some are didactic.[3]

The table dimension of the Eucharist appears in Ignatius' description of the deacons in his letter to the Trallians (2:1): "Furthermore, it is necessary that those who are deacons of the 'mysteries' of Jesus Christ please everyone in every respect. For they are not merely 'deacons' of food and drink, but ministers of God's church."[4] The deacons apparently served the food at meals, perhaps even the Eucharistic meal ("mysteries" is probably an allusion to the Eucharist). It appears that the "love feast" (*agape*) and the Eucharist were still held together. No baptism or "love feast" (fellowship meal), according to the letter to the Smyrneans (8:2), is authorized without the approval of the bishop. The passage describes the two most important functions of a bishop, that is, to oversee baptisms and Eucharists.

However, Ignatius fills his descriptions of the Eucharist with altar language. For example, he encourages the Philadelphians (4) to "participate in one Eucharist" which "is one flesh" and "one cup," just as there is "one altar" and "one bishop."[5] Sacrificial language is important to Ignatius because he sees his own coming martyrdom as an imitation of Jesus' own sacrifice (*Romans* 2:2; 4:2). His life is a sacrifice. Indeed, the "one altar" is Jesus Christ (*Magnesians* 7:2). This contextualizes Ignatius description of the Eucharist with sacrificial language. Consequently, he describes the assembled church as the "place of sacrifice" (*entos tou thysiasteriou*; *Ephesians* 5:2; cf. *Magnesians* 7:2; *Traillians* 7:2; *Philadelphians* 4). Ignatius' intent is to locate the place where Jesus resides, the place of communion and reconciliation. Wherever Jesus is, the altar is. Thus, the Eucharist of the assembled church is closely associated with the altar because it is closely associated with the flesh and blood of Jesus. When the church comes together in one place, it comes to eat the Eucharist and to commune with the flesh and blood of Jesus (*Ephesians* 5:3; 13:1; *Magnesians* 7:1;

Philadelphians 6:2, 10:1). Later Cyprian of Carthage (ca. 250) would interpret this altar language as the actual re-sacrificing of the Christ in the Eucharist (*Letters* 63.9, 17).6

By the time of Justin Martyr (ca. 150s), the bread and wine were totally separated from the meal (table). He only mentions the bread and wine (*First Apology*, 67). The *Agape* meal had become a separate entity celebrated at a different time. The Roman apologist Minucius Felix (ca. 160), a contemporary of Justin Martyr, describes *Agape* feasts in the mid-second century (*Octavius* 31:5). Indeed, that Christians gathered together at religious meals is pictured in the famous *Fractio Panis* fresco in a Roman catacomb (seven participants reclining at a table with five loaves of bread and two fish). The *Fractio Panis* probably pictures an *Agape* which included the Eucharist.

At the end of the second century, Clement of Alexandria often comments on *Agape* feasts (cf. *Paidagogos* 2:1-5). Contemporary with Clement of Alexandria, Tertullian of Carthage describes how the church would meet on Sunday evening to eat a meal with prayer and praise (singing). It was designed to feed the poor in the church (*Apology* 39). Some fifty years later, Cyprian describes the celebration of the Eucharist in morning assemblies as most appropriate to its meaning (*Letters* 63.15-16). *Agape* feasts are celebrated throughout the rest of the day (*Letters* 1.16). Cyprian successfully separated the Eucharist as a morning liturgical/ecclesial event from the *Agape* as a domestic (home-based) evening event.

By the middle of the third century, then, the separation of Eucharist from the meal was complete. The Eucharist was generally celebrated in the morning and the *Agape* in the evening. More and more the Eucharist became associated with altar language, while the table imagery was generally used to describe the *Agape*. The two were separated as the latter was subject to abuse (as in Corinth) and the former was increasingly shaped by an altar atmosphere. Further, as worship assemblies moved to mornings, the *Agape* remained in the evening. The Eucharist belonged to the morning assembly because it was the time of the resurrection, but the table as a meal belonged to the evening *Agape*. The Eucharist was restricted to baptized believers, but the poor, widows (cf. *Didaskalia* 9), and others in the community were invited to the *Agape*. Ultimately, the Eucharist became a liturgical event in the assembly of the church, and the *Agape* was a benevolent, ministry event outside of the formal assembly of the church. What was united in the New Testament, the sharing of food as *koinonia* with the needy and poor in the Lord's supper, is divided in the early centuries of the church.

The *Agape* continued in the early church for several centuries in various forms, though problems with abuse continued. Three councils in the fourth century attempted to correct abuses (Council of Gangra in 353 A.D, Council of Laodicea in 363 A.D., and Council of Carthage in 393 A.D.). The 27th canon of the Council of Laodicea (Canon 28) forbade the practice of the *Agape* in the church building, even forbidding the use of tables. By the end of the seventh century, *Agape* feasts had disappeared and the "table" dimension of the church had totally dissipated. The Trullen Council of 692 repeated the prohibition of *Agape* meals in the church building (including tables). By the end of the eighth century, *Agape* meals were no longer part of the Western church.

The primary impetus for the division between the Eucharist and the *Agape* is the shift from home-based (domestic) meetings to church-based (ecclesial) meetings. Indeed, Cyprian argues that since the whole church must be gathered for the Eucharist, it is no longer feasible to meet in homes since not everyone could gather there. Thus, a meal is no longer practical for the Eucharist (*Letters* 63.16). As the church gained increasing acceptance and grew in numbers, it began to secure its own special meeting places ("church buildings"). These became the norm after Constantine made Christianity a legal religion and ultimately Christianity became the only legal reli-gion by the end of the fourth century (hence, "the Constantinian Shift"[7]). The move from home to church facilitated the move from table to altar. The church setting reshaped the context of the Lord's supper. Table no longer had a function in the church building; indeed, tables were ultimately forbidden. Rather, altar became the focal point. This changed the practice, mood and atmosphere of the Lord's supper. The form of the supper reshaped its function. It was no longer a table, but an altar.

Renewal of Table

The loss of the table in the early centuries and the total dis-solution of the *Agape* in the seventh century recontextualized the Lord's supper for the next thirteen centuries. Altar, rather than table, is the dominant form of the Lord's supper among Christian traditions. Few have seriously attempted to renew the table because it necessitates a highly critical stance toward tra-dition (in this case centuries of tradition) and a strong primi-tivist (restorationist) impulse.

However, some have sought table renewal at various times. For example, the *Unitas Fratrum* of the 1450s in Bohemia (Moravians) engaged in communal practices based on Acts 2. They shared property and abolished social-economic distinc-tions in their community. They shared a daily evening *Agape* and apparently partook of bread and wine as part of the event.

The Brethren movement in its various forms (Church of the Brethren, the Dunkard Brethren, Old German Baptist Brethren, the Brethren Church and the Fellowship of Grace Brethren Churches), which originated in late seventeenth century, includ-ed communion in the context of an *Agape*. Some (Dunkard Brethren and Old German Baptist Brethren) practice the *Agape* as the only legitimate form of communion.[8]

The Quaker tradition, which began in the seventeenth cen-tury, renewed the table dimension of the Lord's supper. In fact, they collapsed the Lord's supper into every meal. All meals are the Lord's meals.

In the mid-seventeenth century, the Scottish Church began to observe "communion festivals" at tables. Participants sat a long tables as if they were sitting for a meal. They ate large portions of bread and drank wine as if they were at a meal. All that was missing was the actual meal itself. Eventually these festivals became three and four day events where thousands communed at tables. The Cane Ridge revival in August, 1801, which between ten and twenty thousand people attended, was designed as a communal festival.[9]

Arising out of these strands of Moravian, Brethren and Scottish table events, British dissenters (e.g., John Glas, 1695-1773 and Robert Sandeman, 1718-1771) restored the *Agape* to the mid-eighteenth century separated churches in England and Scotland. Circular letters, for example, from a Scotch Baptist congregation in New York and a dissenter church in Manchester, England described the love feast as a regular part of their Sunday observance.[10] In 1985 a modern Glasite church still existed in Edinburgh and the *Agape* feast was still part of their Sunday observance.[11]

Against this background of Scottish communion festivals and the British dissenters (particularly Sandemanians), Alexander Campbell re-emphasized the "table" in his teaching about the breaking of bread. Campbell argued typologically that "in the house of God there is always a table of the Lord."[12] Emphasizing the weekly table, he denied all clerical distinctions and recommended joy as the primary mood of the table: "All Christians are members of the house or family of God, are called and constituted a holy and a royal priesthood, and may, therefore bless God for the Lord's table, its loaf, and cup—approach it without fear and partake of it with joy as often as they please, in remembrance of the death of their Lord and Saviour."[13] The table was so central for Campbell that when he described his ideal "meeting-house" he substituted the table for the pulpit. His "meeting-house" would have no pulpit, but "the Lord's table and the seats for the elders of the congregation" would "be at the remote end, opposite to the entrance" and the disciples would be placed "immediately contiguous to the Lord's table."[14]

When Campbell provided a kind of "model" assembly for saints on Sunday, the table was at the center. He describes an assembly of 50 saints with two elders where disciples sat on either side of the table. He was impressed with the "easy, familiar, solemn, cheerful" manner of the table as there was "no stiffness, no formality, no pageantry."[15] It was a simple table where disciples ate with the living Lord. The disciples actually gathered around a table rather than sitting in rows of pews before a pulpit. This was Campbell's fundamental conception of the table. However, though Campbell thought the *Agape* feast was a worthy element of the "restoration of the ancient order," he did not think it was linked to the Lord's supper.[16]

The table-centeredness of the American Restoration Movement (Stone-Campbell Movement) was a distinctive of the tradition. "Gathering around the table" was common—not just as a metaphor, but the physical presence around the table. Tables were more important than pulpits. When Moses Lard described his ideal church, the table extended "entirely across the house" as everyone gathered around the table and partook standing as a sign of reverence.[17] Table-renewal was part of the original vision of the Stone-Campbell Movement, but it was lost in the focus on the elements (leavened or unleavened bread, wine or grape juice) and frequency of the supper (only on Sunday and every Sunday). Losing the tableness of the supper, the movement defaulted to the historic Christian idea of "altar." While we talked about "the Lord's table," little in our assemblies resembled a table. Instead, the atmosphere, function and practice of the supper was decidedly "altar." Even though we often spoke of "gathering around the table," we no longer actually did.

Conclusion

At the conclusion of his piece on the significance of the Lord's supper, Marlin Jeschke writes:

> I would like to test the straightforward suggestion that we seriously consider returning to the agape meal, that is, the full meal form of communion. Not a few voices are calling for this today. I know that this suggestion will run into serious opposition in many quarters. This is so not only because of inertia and stubbornness in congregations. This is also so because of a general impression among us, as in other Protestant churches, that somehow our particular tradition finished the work of the Reformation; we removed all unbiblical accretions of church history and restored our church to pristine Christianity. We stoutly resist the suggestion that there may be some points on which the Reformation never did get completed.
>
> My claim is that a candid review of the story of the Lord's supper shows that, for whatever reason, *on this matter the believers church movement, with the exception of our Brethren friends, did not return the church to New Testament patterns.* We need to continue the Reformation. Our restorationist convictions should make us, especially us believers church people, open to the idea of respecting the model of the New Testament, when that model is explained and called for.[18]

If the form of the supper has any significance, a return to the table is important. The table dimension of the Lord's supper, and thus the communal idea of fellowship and shared food, was lost in the history of the church. Locating the meaning of the supper as an altar in a church building radically altered the practice of the supper. Even as some Protestant churches, especially in the believers church traditions, dismissed the altar language, the practice of the supper was still shaped by an altar mentality.

Radical restoration is necessary in order to restore the table. But this is not about "restoring patterns" or ecclesiological structures. On the contrary, this is about retrieving the original intent and meaning of the supper itself. What was originally "table fellowship" along the trajectory of Old Testament fellowship meals, Jesus' meals with people, and the future messianic banquet became an individualistic altar. To restore the table is not about restoring a mandated form according to some blueprint. To restore the table is to restore the divine intent and function of the Lord's supper. Since form shapes function, in order to restore the function of the supper the contemporary church should return to its original form as table. The church must find the meaning of the supper at Jesus' table. The Lord's supper must become a real table fellowship if it is to recover its original function.

Questions for Discussion

1. Which part of the historical survey did you find most interesting or surprising?

2. How did the shift from "home" to "church building" affect the church's practice of the Lord's supper? How does it affect other dimensions of our ecclesial life?

3. How did the shift from "table" to "altar" affect the church's understanding of the Lord's supper?

4. Should the church be "table-centered" or "word-centered" in its worship? Or both? How would either affect the practice of the supper in your congregation?

10 / THE THEOLOGICAL MEANING OF THE TABLE

Summarizing the theological meaning of the table within the short space of a brief chapter is a daunting task. It is difficult to be comprehensive yet specific, and it is difficult to decide what to emphasize or even how to summarize such a multi-perspective reality as the Lord's supper.

I have often remarked that there is not a biblical sermon which could not be linked in some way with the Lord's supper. This has seemed strange to many because there are so few texts that explicitly discuss the Lord's supper. However, if one grasps the multi-perspective character of the theology embedded in the Lord's supper, it is rather facile to link the sermon to the supper through a theological motif. This is true because the supper is the gospel in bread and wine. As a gospel event it embodies all that the gospel is. Thus, whenever the gospel is proclaimed, the supper gives concrete, visible expression to the message of the gospel through eating and drinking.

The table proclaims the good news of Jesus Christ. It proclaims his atoning work and his resurrection victory. It proclaims God's judgment upon those who reject his offer of grace but it also welcomes all who come in faith. It proclaims hope, but also proclaims the finality of God's work in Christ. Even as it includes, it excludes those who set themselves against the gospel. It visibly unites the people of God and gives expression to their fellowship with each other and with God. The supper proclaims the gospel.

In this chapter, I will summarize the theology of the supper from two basic perspectives. First, I will interpret the theology of the supper from the perspective of its function as a covenant meal. Second, I will interpret the theology of the supper from the perspective of the work of God in Christ. The former is more slanted toward understanding the supper through redemptive-historical eyes (that is, the narrative unity of Scripture as covenant), but the latter positions the meaning of the supper in the context of Christian systematic theology (that is, its Christological meaning in the context of the Christian worldview). While there is some overlap in this approach, the differing perspectives illuminate the theology of the supper in multiple ways.

The Covenantal Character of the Table[1]

One of the most fruitful ways of revitalizing the experience of the Lord's supper today is a thorough understanding of its covenantal meaning. The context of such a covenantal understanding is the Old Testament covenant meal (chapter two). The table is no mere symbolic eating of a pinch of bread and a sip of wine. Rather, it is a full banquet with rich food and drink. The experience of covenant is a table experience.

Covenantal Memory. When we remember Christ in the Lord's supper, we remember the covenant God has made with his people. The spiritual reality of this covenant is actualized for us through our remembering. It moves from a past memory to a present experience of the reality of God's grace. The bread and wine actualize the reality of salvation for us in the worship experience. There is a genuine experience of salvation when we eat and drink by faith. To remember God's work in Christ is to experience the reality of our covenantal fellowship with God. It is not mere cognitive reflection. The spiritual reality of God's salvation is present through our remembering. The Lord's supper, then, is a moment of grace when we receive it by faith through our memory of God's work for us.

Covenantal Renewal. When we eat and drink we renew our covenant with God. We pledge ourselves to keep the covenant. Just as Israel voiced its willingness to obey the covenant, so we ratify the covenant in our life when we eat and drink. It is a moment of rededication and recommitment. In the context of the worship experience, we voice our commitment to live worthy of the gospel (cf. Phil. 1:27). We vow to take up our cross, call Jesus Lord and follow him into the world as obedient servants. The supper is the ritual moment when we renew the covenant vow we made in our baptism.

Covenantal Presence. God has always promised to live among his people and to be their God (cf. Gen. 17:7-8; Lev. 26:11-12; Jer. 11:4; 24:7). God is present among his people in the covenant meal—it is an eating and drinking in the presence of the covenant Lord (Ex. 18:12; Deut. 12:7,18; 14:23-26; 15:20; 1 Chron. 29:22). The presence of God in the meal as in the tabernacle and temple is a covenantal presence. This presence is found in the church through the indwelling Spirit by whom we are the temple of God (1 Cor. 3:16; 6:19; 2 Cor. 6:16), and by whom the Living Lord is present through faith (Eph. 3:16,17). The church is the habitation of God through the Spirit (Eph. 2:22). In the covenant meal, the body and blood of Christ are present through the Spirit who lifts us up to share the spiritual reality rooted in Christ. As we worship in the Spirit (Phil. 3:3), Christ is present through the covenant meal. Christ is the living host who serves his people at the table. The presence of Christ is his presence at the table, not his presence in the bread and wine. He hosts and serves his table and is thereby present among his people when they eat and drink together.

Covenantal Fellowship. The covenant meal symbolizes and mediates the fellowship between God and his covenant people. It testifies to the reconciliation which God has enacted and the peace which exists between God and the redeemed, and between the redeemed. It is a moment of joy, communion and thanksgiving. The people of God celebrate their reconciliation by God's work; they rejoice in the redemptive work of God for them. The covenant meal is a Eucharist, a thanksgiving, which assures the worshipper of God's love and redemptive work. As surely as one eats and drinks through faith, so also one certainly participates in God's salvation and in the community of God.

The Lord's supper is not something to be avoided in times of doubt and uncertainty; it is a gracious gift to be received by faith where doubt and uncertainty can be eradicated by the testimony of God's covenant in the meal. It is a testament of his love. It is a moment of communal fellowship between God and his community. It is a moment of communion with the risen Lord at whose table we eat and drink. Further, it is not only a fellowship between God and the community, but it is a communal fellowship within the community. When the community sits at table together, it shares the same reality (Christ) and is united by their common faith. The common table visibly bears witness to the "common union" of those who sit at the table. It is a fellowship between believers as well as with God.

Covenantal Promise. The new covenant meal is one of hope and expectation. We live in the light of God's revelation of the end of history—he showed us what the end of history is through the resurrection of Jesus. The Lord's supper, then, is a celebration of God's victory over death through Jesus. It is not a funeral, but a celebratory affirmation of hope in a tragic, fallen world. Through the covenant meal we proclaim our faith in God's eschatological promises, and we anticipate the messianic banquet in God's eschatological kingdom. As we eat and drink now, we eat and drink in the hope of eating and drinking with Jesus in the fullness of his kingdom.

The Gospel Character of the Supper

The symbolism of the supper is directly linked with the gospel event. The objective event of the supper re-presents the gospel of Christ. It is not just a sign, but a means. It is a participation in the death and resurrection of Jesus. It is a means of concrete spiritual communion with Christ. Genuine spiritual communion and relation with Christ is experienced in the context of this objective event. There is power in the supper: through faith there is forgiveness, power for living and assurance in the present. The redemptive-historical event is linked to our own personal history. We are assured of our link to Christ, our link to his historical act on our behalf, through eating and drinking with him.

The supper is experienced in an assembly—not necessarily a "church building" assembly, but among the gathered people of God. The supper is communal worship. Worship is a sanctifying experience—it is an entrance into the holy presence of God which renews, sanctifies and sends us out for service. It is a moment of transformation and empowerment. The Lord's supper, along with the Word, as the central focus of the worship of early Christians testifies to this meaning. It is where we meet God—where we "see" him and commune with the risen Christ. The risen Christ is our host as we commune with him in the supper. We eat and drink in God's presence, and that moment is a holy one because God, the holy one, is present among his people for this meal.

Worship on the Lord's day, in celebration of the resurrection of Jesus, is a community event. It is a holy time/space for the community. At the center of that holy time/space is the proclamation of the gospel in word and deed—through preaching and eating/drinking.

The Gracious Character of the Lord's Supper. The supper is a moment through which God graciously communes with his people; it is a moment of holy presence among his people. This is both a sign and a means by which the transcendent God dwells among his people as Covenant Lord who sits as host at his covenant meal.

The gracious character of the moment is God's invitation to sit at his table and enjoy his fellowship. It is not just a memory of a past gracious act, but it is the present experience of God's grace through Jesus Christ. When the supper is human-centered and human-focused—when it is conceived merely on a horizontal level—then it has lost its fundament root. The supper is a vertical as well as a horizontal experience.

The supper, like baptism, is first and foremost God's act. He invites us to his table where he hosts our communal fellowship. We only have horizontal fellowship because God has vertically established fellowship with him. We have fellowship with each other because our fellowship is in him. Unfortunately, some traditions have so emphasized the horizontal dimension that the supper has become androcentric in focus. It has become more about what we do (our obedience, duty, memory, etc.) than what God does. Some have turned the supper into mere human obedience rather than understanding it primarily as God's divine act of grace. The supper is first and foremost God's act through which he communes with us and unites his people into one body around the table.

The Ecclesiological Nature of the Lord's Supper. Though a divine act, the supper has ecclesial and communal import. It is the public confession/proclamation of the church. It is our witness to the world that we believe in the good news of the death and resurrection of Jesus Christ. It is a confession of our sinfulness. It is our public recognition that we need the expiatory sacrifice of Jesus Christ and that we are unworthy to receive the grace that God is willing to give. Yet, we make this confession with joy because the supper is a testimony to divine forgiveness. The body and blood of Christ mean that God redeems his people and establishes communion with them. When we come to table, we come in humility but with a peace that comes from God's gracious declaration in the gospel as proclaimed by the table.

It is the public symbol and expression of the unity of the church. The one body eats the one bread and drinks the one cup. We are united in the name of Jesus Christ as God's unique mediator between us and him. When we sit at the table with each other, we demonstrate God's love for the diversity of humanity who now sit at the same table. Rich and poor, Jew and Gentile, slave and free, black and white, male and female sit at the table together in the presence of God. Diverse humanity is now united in a concrete moment of table fellowship.

It is the public renewal of the covenant. We rededicate and reaffirm our discipleship in this covenant meal. We invoke a covenant curse upon ourselves so that should we ever forsake the covenant, we eat and drink damnation upon ourselves. The Lord's supper is a serious moment because it involves a serious commitment to follow Jesus. We eat as disciples and when we eat we reaffirm our vow of discipleship. Thus, in this meal, like the vow offering in the Old Testament, we make a pledge. We pledge to follow Jesus as we sit at his table in his kingdom.

It is an identification with the people of God over against the world. The fundamental environment of the covenant meal is communal. It is taken in community as a community. It should not reflect factions and schisms in the body, but should unite the body. As a communal event it is the symbol of the body's unity itself. Individualistic interpretations of the Lord's supper as some kind of private moment between God and an individual obscure the essential communal character of the event. While the Lord's supper is both a vertical (communion God) and horizontal event (communion with each other), in

the New Testament its context, like its Old Testament ante-
cedents, is fundamentally communal.

It is the public commitment of the church to mission and
service. As the church eats at the table of the incarnate servant
of God, so the church is committed to emulate his service. At the
table the church embodies the mission of Jesus as it invites everyone to the table and serves them. The supper is a proclamation
of the gospel. It binds the church to the mission of the gospel.

The Ethical Nature of the Lord's Supper. Because the supper
involves covenant renewal and an expression of covenant commitment, it expresses an understanding of covenantal obliga-
tions. Just as the covenant meal meant a dedication and commitment to the Lord, so does the Lord's supper. Paul makes this
explicit application in 1 Corinthians 10. Idolatry will evoke the
Lord's jealousy. One should not eat at the table of demons and
at the table of the Lord. To eat the Lord's table is to commit
oneself to his cause, his fellowship and his Lordship. And one
cannot have two masters or two Lords. The Lord's supper, then,
reflects our ethical commitment to serve the Lord.

The supper ought to overcome social polarizations within
a congregation. Paul describes several in Corinth, such as
strong and weak, rich and poor, Jew and Gentile, and male and
female. Different groups threaten to divide the church, and
some are socially motivated (rich/poor) and others are functions of elitism (knowledgeable vs. unlearned). The supper
calls the church to transcend such distinctions so as to unite in
one moment of communion at the table of Christ. The supper
ought to reflect the unity of the community rather than be an
occasion for the prevailing cultural, social and economic differences to divide it. The manner in which the supper is conducted ought to reflect the values and ethics of Jesus Christ. Our
table fellowship must be patterned after his. Consequently, who
do we invite to the table and with whom do we choose to eat?
We should invite the oppressed, the poor, the handicapped to

sit at the table in order to show the "kindness of God" to them (the example of David's relationship to Mephibosheth in 2 Sam. 9:1-3; cf. Lk. 14:15-24).

The ecclesial function of the supper was most vividly demonstrated in the Jerusalem church. There the supper had an economic function as the church shared their food and possessions as a function of *koinonia*. When the disciples ate together, they shared their food with the needy. As Yoder comments, "bread eaten together is economic sharing."[1] The earliest disciples fellowshipped through the sharing of food and goods; they "had all things in common" (*koina*; Acts 2:44). Thus, the supper testifies to how the community is committed to mutual sharing just as God has shared with them through the body and blood of his Son.

The Eschatological Nature of the Lord's Supper. We participate in the supper looking toward the hope of the new heaven and the new earth. We proclaim Christ in the light of his coming, as we anticipate it. It is a realized eschatology which anticipates the full messianic banquet in the eschaton. We eat with the Lord at his table where he sits as the living host as we anticipate the eschatological messianic banquet where we will see the face of God.

This perspective should shape the practice of the supper in the church. Since we eat in hope and in anticipation of the coming banquet, we do not eat with remorse or sadness. We do not sit at a funeral banquet, but a messianic banquet. We eat with joy as we await the future victory over death through our own resurrection. We anticipate the fullness of God's victory when he will wipe away all tears and destroy death. Thus, eating and drinking is a hopeful, joyous experience. When we eat and drink, we pray for the kingdom to come. We voice, with the early church, "Marnatha," that is, "Our Lord, come!" (1 Cor. 16:22).

Conclusion

The Lord's supper is God's gracious presence among his people. As a gospel event, God takes the initiative and graciously offers himself in communion with his people. The supper is God's gracious, reconciling and forgiving presence. God does not come in judgment to those who sit at the table by faith. Rather, he comes in assurance and grace. As surely as the church eats the bread and drinks the cup, as surely as it sits at table with the Lord, so the certainty of salvation is assured to the fellowship of believers. When we eat and drink, we can boldly proclaim that "Jesus is ours." Primarily the supper is a divine act rather than a human one. God graciously works hope, assurance and peace in our hearts at the table. Thus, instead of running from the table because of our fear of unworthiness, in faith we should run to the table because there we are assured of God's grace in Jesus Christ.

The Lord's supper is our grateful response in covenantal commitment. While the supper is a divine act, it is nevertheless also a human one. It is a human affirmation of covenantal commitment and thanksgiving. When we eat and drink, we commit ourselves to the values of the gospel which the supper embodies. We offer thanks for divine grace. Through the supper we commit ourselves to God and to each other. When we sit at table with the Lord who served the table, we commit ourselves to serve tables. When we sit at table with the Lord who humbled himself to give his life for others, we commit ourselves to the humble service of others, even to the point of giving our lives (and stuff!) for each other. Eating and drinking without commitment is to eat and drink judgment, but to eat and drink with commitment is to visibly take up your cross at the table and follow Jesus.

The Lord's supper is a fellowship of Divine Host with human guests. God comes to his people at the table. He is genuinely present through the living host, Jesus Christ. It is no mere symbolic fellowship, but an encounter with the Living God. That encounter generates joy, peace, and hope as it remembers the victory of God over the grave in the resurrection of Jesus and anticipates the coming messianic banquet. The present table is a foretaste of the eschatological table in the new heaven and new earth where God will fully dwell with his people as their God. There the goal of God is fully accomplished and God sits at table with his people as he always intended.

Questions for Discussion

1. What are the implications for categorizing the Lord's supper as a "covenant meal"? How might your congregation enhance this theological feature in its practice of the Lord's supper?

2. What is the "gospel character" of the Lord's supper? How might your congregation enhance this theological character in its practice of the Lord's supper?

3. Is there tension between the gracious witness of the supper and the expectation of covenantal commitment ("eating worthily")?

4. Given the multi-perspectival character of the supper, is it realistic to think that any sermon (homily on the Word of God) might find concrete connection in the supper? Why or why not? Illustrate.

11 / THE PRACTICE OF THE TABLE IN THE CONTEMPORARY CHURCH

Because the supper is a holy, serious and theologically meaningful event, its practice is revered and valued. It is "holy communion." Christians invest tremendous importance in the supper. As a long established ritual in Christian assemblies, the supper is associated with many traditional elements. The order, context and atmosphere of the supper is solidly entrenched in most congregations. Specific ways of observing the supper have been part of some congregations for generations. Consequently, any change in practice is met with resistance because it upsets long standing piety.

While this piety should be honored and valued for the way it has engendered and nurtured faith among the people of God, some aspects of that piety may hinder a fuller appreciation and experience of the intended function of the supper. Tradition is important as it gives form and shape to biblical theology. When it provides stability, continuity and identity to God's people, tradition serves a valid and necessary function. But that tradition must reflect and embody the fullness of biblical theology. When tradition truncates, or even distorts, the meaning of the supper, the biblical values should reshape the tradition. In this instance, the church should creatively embody those values through beginning new traditions. No church can exist without traditions. They are necessary for stability and continuity. However, those traditions should always be "revisioned" through the eyes of biblical values.

In this chapter I will suggest some fairly significant changes in our contemporary practice of the supper. My suggestions are not rooted in a love for change. Change is neither inherently good nor evil. Change which reforms the practice of the church so that it more closely exhibits biblical values is good, but change that promotes ambition or novelty is evil. Consequently, every change in the practice of the supper must conform to its theological meaning and embody that meaning in the contemporary church. In particular, the church should display the multi-perspective character of the supper and practice it with rich diversity rather than with the formalism of a single ritual form.

The Abiding Presence of an Altar Mentality

The predominant atmosphere of the supper in the contemporary church is an altar mentality. The church usually approaches the supper with penance and confession of sin. We come to the "altar" with our guilt and remorse, or we come to the "altar" with deep introspection. We are encouraged to think about the death of Christ, especially its pain and gore. We are told to concentrate on the meaning of Christ's atonement and focus our attention solely on what Christ did on the cross. From childhood we are socialized to eat the supper in silent contemplative prayer or meditation. No one talks while they eat and drink. No one looks up but everyone prays with a bowed head, and certainly no one looks anyone else in the eye. The altar is a time for private, silent meditation on the cross of Christ. In practice, the table became an altar in the church. We still use the language of "table," but we practice it as an altar.

This altar mentality is not the possession of only one tradition in Christian history. It is just the opposite. The altar mentality is the common possession of the whole Christian tradition with few exceptions. It began early and was formalized in static rituals in the fourth and fifth centuries. The contemporary church has inherited the altar mentality from centuries of Christian tradition.

But as we have surveyed the biblical materials, the table metaphor is more than figurative language. It was a real table as Christians gathered for a meal where they shared themselves and their food in the presence of the living host. The table, as a meal, was an interactive event where people talked with each other and "fellowshipped" each other. They not only shared food, but they shared their lives. Rather than private introspection, the table was a public, expressive and communal event. Rather than approached in penance, sorrow and remorse, people experienced the table with joy and peace. Rather than feeling remorse for what Christ had to do on the cross because of our sin, the table was a celebrative thanksgiving meal for what God did in Christ. It expressed commitment more than penance. Table was more about eating and drinking with the risen Lord than it was a gruesome remembrance of the death of Christ. We remember the death of Christ with joy because it is good news for sinners and the resurrection transforms apparent defeat into victory. The table celebrates victory.

The contrast between an altar mentality and a table mentality is illustrated in the chart below. While the contrasts can be overdrawn (e.g., there are times when a table is characterized by sorrow because the community is surround by tragedy, as, for example, the Sunday after 9-11), the biblical-theological emphasis is the experience of the table as depicted in the chart.

Altar	*Table*
Silent	Interactive
Solemn	Celebrative
Individual	Communal
Sorrow	Joy
Remorse	Thanksgiving
Contemplative	Fellowship
Introspective	Expressive
Penance	Commitment
Focused on Death	Focused on Resurrection

There is a connection between the altar (the cross) and the table (Lord's supper). At the table we enjoy the benefits of the altar. We enjoy the reconciliation and peace which the altar procured. But when we are at the table, we are no longer at the altar. The altar is about blood and death rituals, but the table is about life. At the table, we remember what Christ did at the altar, but we do not remember with remorse or sadness. We remember with thanksgiving and joy. We give thanks for the body and blood of Christ.

Consistently, the biblical witness is a joyous table. No table in the Old or New Testament is burdened with sadness. Tables are always about reconciliation, peace and joy. Even the Last Supper, on the night Jesus was betrayed, was filled with love (washed feet), joy (anticipating the kingdom of God, even to the point of arguing over who would be the greatest), and fellowship (eating the Passover together).

Even altars were occasions of great joy in the Hebrew sacrificial ritual because they were atonement offerings which secured peace between God and his people. For example, the morning and evening burnt offerings were accompanied with trumpets, musical instruments and songs of praise (1 Chron. 16:39-42). But the altar mentality is something that was fostered, in its most dominant form, by the medieval church which viewed the Mass as primarily penitential. It is this private, penitential focus on the death of Christ that characterizes the modern church and it is precisely this that is so contrary to the table environment and meaning of the Lord's supper. The task for the contemporary church is to revision the supper as table in a way that refocuses the supper on the resurrection of Jesus rather than his death; to refocus the supper on life, peace, joy and victory.

Revisioning the Supper as Table

Actually sitting at a table in our assemblies is generally impractical. Our "auditoriums" were designed as lecture halls more than fellowship halls. The arrangement of the pews lacks a communal sense because we are unable to see each other much less sit with each other at table. Instead of sitting across from one another at a table, we look at the back of each other's heads. There is little or no eye contact with other believers in our assemblies and especially during the Lord's supper where such eye contact is discouraged.

Moreover, usually the size of the church renders any kind of real table impractical. Not only would space cause a problem (most churches do not have the space to accommodate their whole congregation at tables in a single meal), but logistically it is difficult for 200 to 500 people, and especially 2500, to eat a meal together with any kind of intimacy and sense of shared experience. Such meals either become too chaotic or too formal.

Consequently, larger congregations which want to shift from an altar to table face a difficult task. How can a congregation of 250 in a traditional "pewed" auditorium, for example, experience the Lord's supper as table? Without a real table, how can a congregation experience the communal, celebrative and interactive intent of the Lord's table? Below are several suggestion. Some are small adjustments, others are more significant. Some are minor changes, but others are major. None, of course, are prescriptive, but their intent is to foster a table mentality in contrast to an altar mentality.

There are several simple suggestions, which many are implementing across the country, that encourage a communal perspective. For example, singing together during the supper highlights the fact that this is a shared experience. Others read Scripture as the supper is distributed within the assembly. Still others encourage people to hold the bread and cup until everyone has been served so that everyone can eat and drink at the same time.

Worship planners should give more attention to the transitions within the assembly. For example, the connection between Word and table needs more specific attention. How does the Word shape the table and how does the table illustrate and embody the Word? The songs, readings and prayers associated with the supper will contribute to the shared experience as participants reflect on the same themes together. Consequently, some songs between the elements, as well as during the distribution of the elements, help this focus. But also communal prayer readings give concrete expression to the communal character of the table. Instead of one prayer leader, let the congregation read a communal prayer together or engage in a responsive reading/prayer so that the congregation is more participatory than silently listening to the reading or prayer of another.

The leadership should give explicit permission to look around at others with whom they are eating the supper. Given our socialization in the etiquette of the Lord's supper, people need that permission. Yet, "pew" etiquette means that one should not "look around" at others. But this is exactly where our "pew" architecture and the meaning of the table diverge because when you are at table with someone, you cannot avoid looking at them (unless you are quite rude!). Further, "looking around" in silence does not really approximate the table either. Consequently, people should be encouraged to speak to the person next to them. They could share a prayer together or offer a word about what the gospel means in their lives. This, of course, is not a silent prayer, but verbal. Indeed, several people on a row could lean over to pray together as the elements are distributed. Or, they could simply encourage each other in the name of Jesus: "This body is for you," or "Jesus has forgiven you of your sins," or "Peace be with you." Worship leaders should encourage believers to speak with each other during this time, perhaps even suggesting the topic of conversation or the words they should repeat to each other.

At the corporate level, the leadership could encourage testimonies in the midst of the supper. One or more could share their personal stories of grace and reconciliation as the supper is distributed or prior to its distribution. Just as in the Old Testament thanksgiving meals, so at the Lord's supper we can corporately celebrate God's goodness to one of his people as we eat and drink together. Testimonies about the supper would also facilitate the communal dimension of the table. For example, ask some new Christians to express what the supper means to them, or ask some older members to express what it means to them as they reflect on their history with God.

Another way to emphasize table is to have four or five tables set up throughout the assembly room. Instead of eating from their pew, disciples get up and go to one of the tables in the room, or the whole congregation goes to one table in the assembly. Perhaps they gather around it or they come in twos or threes to the table to eat together. Families might come to the table and eat as families (we must be careful, however, to include singles in our invitation in a way that they feel part of the community and eat with a group). Or, ask everyone to gather around one of the tables and stand there together. The bread and cup are then passed among the group gathered at the table.

In smaller churches, I have asked everyone to come down around the table, that is, to literally "gather around the table" to eat and drink together. As we stand around the table, we pass the bread and cup to each other. There are no designated "servers," but rather everyone (women included) serves each other, just like at a table where everyone is seated and passing food.

Another way to emphasize the communal dimension of the table is to ask those who are seated in rows to serve those behind them. When they received the bread and cup, they turn around, serve those seated behind them and eat/drink with them. As they serve each other the bread and cup, they might also greet each other in the name of Jesus, pray with each other, encourage each other and simply share a blessing like "Peace be with you." Indeed, simply asking people to stand as they eat and drink together enhances the communal dimension of the supper since they will be more likely to speak to each other.

There are other possibilities. We need gifted people to understand the theology of the table, the limitations of our present architecture as well as the sizes of our churches, and creatively transform our present "altar" environment into a table one. The biblical value is table, community and joy as we eat and drink together. We should creatively adapt our present realities to the biblical values lest we actually distort the supper rather than celebrate it.

A Supper for Tabled Assemblies

Traditional assemblies can only approximate the table environment through some of the above suggestions. Revisioning the Lord's supper may require an experience of actually sitting at tables in order to grasp the radical difference between altar and table. There is something about actually sitting around a table which generates an atmosphere incongruous with the altar mentality. It is rather impossible to sit at a table and engage in private meditation. Indeed, it would be rude to sit at a table with someone only to sit with bowed head in silence.

Such individualism runs counter to the communal nature of a table. It is simply not table etiquette.

If the Lord's supper is a table, the best setting for observing the Lord's supper is a table. The table gives us the experience which should shape our conduct at the supper. Until we sit across from each other at a table, looking each other in the eye and conversing with each other, it is difficult to understand the distinction between table and altar in the conduct and atmosphere of the Lord's supper.

By "tabled assemblies" I mean assemblies which are gathered at tables rather than sitting in pews. This might be an assembly of 200 people who sit at 15-25 tables of 8-12 each in a fellowship hall, or it might be a Bible class of 60 who sit at 5-7 tables. The tables, with 8-12 people, provide an intimacy for the experience of fellowship and mutual edification. This is parallel to the Jerusalem church where 3000 disciples gathered in homes (presumably 20-50 people) to break bread (Acts 2:46). The 3,000 did not eat the Lord's supper in the temple, but in their homes where they could sit at table with each other in the presence of the Living Lord.

Whether it is the corporate assembly of the whole church or a Bible class (and, depending on which, the particulars of my scenario will change), the table shapes the environment of the Lord's supper in a way that moves beyond the altar mentality. Arrange the room with a sufficient number of tables (round tables work best, but rectangular tables are sufficient) where 8-12 people may sit at a table together. With that many people sitting at a table, it will not be silent and do not expect it to be. The point of the table is facilitate fellowship among the disciples of Jesus.

Whether in a corporate worship assembly or a Bible class, it is important to strongly link the Word and table surrounded by praise and drenched in prayer. Word, table, praise and prayer are the substance of the experience that would follow the Last

Supper and the table experience of early Christians. The assembly would begin and end with prayer and praise as the context in which Christians hear the Word and share the table.

At the heart of the experience, however, is the integration of Word and table. The Word should interpret the table and the table should give concrete expression to the preached (taught) Word. In tabled assemblies I suggest that the homily (or Bible class teaching) surround the table. After a period of prayer and praise, a leader should given the homily (or teaching). Of course, this could be any gospel topic, but it may directly relate to the table (e.g., a homily on the Lord's supper). Yet, any gospel topic (redemption, reconciliation, peace, joy, thanksgiving, unity, fellowship, etc.) is easily connected with the table. The homily (teaching) should apply the gospel theme to the context of the table where that theme is concretely and visibly experienced. At the conclusion of "table time," the leader should summarize the theme and its concrete experience, especially how this experience should shape our lifestyle.

During "table time," the integration of Word and table should continue. Each table should have its own bread and juice (or, wine). I prefer one loaf and a pitcher of juice since the symbolism of one loaf reflects the oneness of the body of Christ and the symbolism of pouring the cup reflects the life that was poured out for us as well as our commitment to pour out our lives for Christ and for each other. Prayer, joy and thanksgiving should dominate this time.

The table should be a place for discussion of the themes articulated by the leader. It should function as a small group discussion which eats and drinks together as it talks about the homily (teaching). Someone at the table would pray and break the bread, and later someone one would pray and pour the cup. Surrounding the eating and drinking would be an interactive discussion of the gospel as presented in the homily (teaching). Specifically, the discussion would focus on the meaning of the gospel, how the table reflects that meaning and how that meaning should shape the rest of our lives when we are living out the gospel in the world. The table should also have some time for prayer as participants share some "praises" and "petitions."

This table experience, then, is interactive, communal and didactic. At the table, the community experiences each other as they share their thoughts. They encourage each other, pray with each other and develop a relationship that is difficult to do sitting in pews. There is no silence at this table, and there is no privacy. It is a shared experience in a shared eating and drinking. It is, in other words, a real table rather than a symbolic one.

A Supper for a Home Meal

The Woodmont Hills Family of God in Nashville, Tennessee organized a home-based hospitality experience in order to eat the Lord's supper in the context of a meal. The hospitality groups were formed for the purpose of sharing the Lord's supper as a meal with four to eight families (10-20 people, including children) on a Sunday evening. The groups were based on geography since Woodmont is a regional church of 2500 people. Around 2000 people participated in a hospitality group. The overwhelming response of the church was positive and created a desire to regularly share the Lord's supper in this manner. The only way a large church can share the supper intimately at a table is in small groups. The Jerusalem church experienced this as well—3000 listened to the teaching of the apostles in the temple, but small groups broke bread in homes. Below are the guidelines I provided for the leaders. I have modified these guidelines for inclusion in this book.

The Setting. It is important that everyone (including children) sit at a table. The tables should have a sufficient number of people for adults/children to converse and discuss the meaning of the table together as they eat/drink together. Multiple tables are fine as space dictates, but since you will be leading the whole event, all the tables need to hear what you are saying.

The Emblems. Each table should have a single loaf of bread (leavened or unleavened, though unleavened is traditional and would cause less disruption) and a pitcher of grape juice (with some medium size cups [not tiny communion cups] into which to pour the juice; some might want to use wine, but again the traditional juice would cause less disruption). As participants in this supper, we want to encourage everyone to eat and drink, and not to taste and sip. Encourage participants to eat a significant piece of bread and to drink their whole cup.

The Goal. To experience the Lord's supper as a communal table meal where spiritual communion is highlighted by prayer, praise and discussion.

The Order. Once seated, enjoy a time of singing and praise. Songs would be appropriate at any point, but especially at the beginning and the end. First, seat everyone at a table (including children). Second, ask each person (including children) to introduce themselves. Do you know everyone at your table? Ask them to tell something about themselves other than just their name, or how long they have been at Woodmont, or their work. For example, ask them to tell everyone one of their hobbies or main interests. Use whatever question or focus might be best for your particular group. Third, if you want a time of singing, this would be good place to have a few songs. The words and music for "Come Share the Lord" would be appropriate, as well as songs of hope, joy and thanksgiving.

Fourth, stress the significance of this evening as a commemoration of the Jesus Christ and a communion with him and with each other. Read Acts 2:42-47.[1] Explain the significance of the text (though I am brief here, expand as you see need): "3000 people were immersed on the day of Pentecost. They formed a community that devoted themselves to the teaching of the apostles and to fellowship. We are here tonight for fellowship, and the particular kind of fellowship that these early Christians experienced. They met for the breaking of bread in their homes and for prayers. Tonight we want to break bread together and spend some time in prayer. The Christians in Jerusalem could not do this as 3000 people. Rather, they met in the Temple as a large group, but they met in homes for the breaking of the bread. It was a time of joy and praise as they shared a meal together—as they shared the Lord's meal. Tonight we will eat the Lord's supper as a meal and seek spiritual communion and renewal through God's gift of the supper."

Fifth, begin the meal with a prayer of thanksgiving for this time together and for the meal. Allow time for some general fellowship as the group begins to know each other and gets settled into the meal.

Sixth, early in the meal, after about 5 minutes, take the bread in your hands and ask the table about the meaning of the bread. Ask a child at the table about it significance—you might prepare this child or alert him/her to what you are about to do. When the response comes that it is the "body of Christ," probe further: "What does it mean to eat the body of Christ?" "For what purpose did Jesus give his body for death?" "What should we experience, know, remember or feel as we eat the body of Christ?"

Allow some discussion of these points at the table. Let each table (if you have multiple ones) discuss it on their own. After a period of discussion, as the leader, take the bread, give thanks for it, break and pass it around the table. Let everyone eat (including the children)—everyone at the table is invited to eat. As each one breaks off the bread and hands it to the person next to them, model this saying: "This is the body of Christ which was given for you." Encourage people to take a large piece rather than just a small bite—break off enough to chew or eat for a few minutes, even to eat throughout the rest of the meal.

Seventh, once everyone has broken off a piece and is eating, continue the meal. Encourage everyone to continue to eat the unleavened bread until it is gone. No leftovers are needed. However, you need to guide the conversation at the table. Consequently, lead the table to discuss something like this: "Christ sacrificed his body for us. He gave his life for us so that we might have life together. Now we need to lay down our lives for each other. Tonight we need to lay down our lives for each other in prayer. At this moment, as we eat, we want to make time for prayer requests and needs. Do you have a burden to share tonight, or perhaps someone close to you needs prayer." Go around the table asking for prayer requests as the meal continues (continue eating!). Appoint someone to lead a prayer specifically for those mentioned or share the prayer time between various people at the table.

Eighth, not too long after the prayer for the burdens mentioned at the table, and as the meal nears an end, but before desert (if any), the leader should take the pitcher of juice and ask about its meaning (similar to the bread). Here the emphasis should be on hope and joy—the blood brings forgiveness, and death is conquered by the resurrection. We drink with joy as we drink in hope. Ask for comment on the meaning of the cup. Offer a prayer of thanksgiving. Pour the juice into the cups, or ask someone else to do this. Stress how the blood of Christ was poured out for us in order to bring us hope.

As each receives a cup of juice, ask them to share something God has done in their lives, or something for which they are thankful, or what this means to them in terms of hope, or how this moment is a hopeful event in their lives. How does this drinking together bring hope to our lives? We might say to each other as the cups are passed, "This is the blood of Christ which gives us hope for the future. Drink in hope." As they drink together, allow the table to discuss hope and its meaning in their lives through their sharing even as they continue to eat the meal.

Ninth, serve desert, and spend the last moments of the meal talking about the experience of the supper as a meal. How does this affect our understanding of the supper? How does a real "table" make a difference as we eat the supper? What did you learn about supper or experience at the table that enriched your faith?

Tenth, in conclusion, it would be appropriate to have some time for songs of praise, or perhaps simply conclude with a prayer of thanksgiving for the evening. Request everyone around the table to contribute a "sentence" to the prayer (that is, let everyone speak a word to God of thanksgiving or petition). Just as you passed the bread and juice, let the word of prayer be passed as well.

Conclusion

Why change? I understand the question. We are comfortable with our history, tradition and practices. They are familiar to us. We have grown accustomed to a particular form and it has molded our faith for years.

However, the reasons for change are fundamentally the notions of "reform" and "renewal." By "reform" I mean the need to reinvest the Lord's supper with biblical meanings that have been lost in the altar environment. When we practice the supper in a way that loses, and sometimes denies, the communal function of the supper, then our practice needs reformation. Form matters because form can not only exhibit appropriate values it can deny the meaning of the supper. The Corinthians denied the meaning of gospel (i.e., it transcends the distinction between rich and poor) by their form. As we continue the altar mentality we deny the gospel meaning of table, that is, we deny community. In the modern church we have devised the most individualistic way of partaking of bread and wine possible (even some pre-packaged bread/juice combinations). Our individualism undermines the table fellowship the supper intends.

Consequently, the supper needs reformation in order to restore the biblical practice that embodies the idea of table.

By "renewal" I mean the need to breathe life, through the Spirit of God, into the contemporary practice of the Lord's supper. Some traditions have removed the Lord's supper from the Sunday assembly because they were convinced that the supper is too boring for unchurched people. If it is conducted as altar, then it can be boring and uninteresting to the unchurched. But if it were truly table, the boredom would dissipate. Tables are not usually boring. As table, the Lord's supper need not be boring either.

Others have beaten themselves up because they lack consistency in concentrating on the death of Christ. They lose focus and feel guilty. But at a real table it is difficult to lose focus because there are so many things going on at once. The Lord's table is multi-perspectival—grace, forgiveness, reconciliation, joy, hope, resurrection, atonement, fellowship, community—and consequently encourages a range of emotions, thoughts and feelings. Reinvesting a table mentality in the supper will renew our contemporary practice by bringing new perspectives and experiences into our assemblies.

Reformation and renewal do not come without conflict, but conflict around the table should be minimized as much as possible. The table is about unity, not division. The table is about mutual service, not ambitious agendas. Consequently, change should come slowly and deliberately. The community needs to hear biblical teaching, dialogue with the teachers and participate in the decisions. This process should be bathed in prayer and mutual love as we seek the interest of others rather than our own.

Nevertheless, if we are to revision the supper in accordance with biblical theology, the church will need to seriously consider how to change both our thinking and practice. The supper is a table, not an altar. It should be celebrated as a table, not an altar. To revision the supper is to return to the table where Jesus is the living host and disciples gather to commune with him and each other.

Discussion Questions

1. What is an "altar" mentality in contrast to a "table" mentality? Identify elements in your own congregational practice which might be identified as "altar" or "table."

2. Why is the "altar" mentality so pervasive in contemporary congregations? How has both historic church culture and modern individualistic culture shaped the "altar" mentality?

3. How would sitting around a table change the dynamics of the Lord's supper in your assembly?

4. How might your congregation emphasize "table" in its celebration of the supper even if it cannot sit around actual tables?

5. Which suggestions in the chapter do you think are most valuable? Which do you find most problematic?

12 / SEVEN COMMON QUESTIONS

This brief study has, at times, hurriedly or incidentally addressed some common questions as it surveyed the biblical, theological and practical landscape. Instead of dwelling on those questions at various points, which would have interrupted the flow of the book, I have delayed a specific answer to them till this point. For the convenience of the reader (but at the risk of repetition), I have assembled in one place some of the more common questions in order to address them within the framework of this book's perspectives.

1. May anyone eat and drink? Traditionally, the church has asked whether it should practice open or closed communion. Historically, the church has generally practiced closed communion. For example, in the *Didache* (9.5) only the baptized were permitted to partake. Alexander Campbell would not commune with the unimmersed.[1] He invited only the immersed to gather around the table while others were separated by some kind of divider. Indeed, in many traditions, only those who had undergone a particular process of examination and/or penance were permitted to come to the table. 20th century Churches of Christ have generally practiced a middle ground as they neither invite nor debar anyone. Each one individually decides whether to eat and drink. The church does not make that decision for anyone. It is an individual decision.

There are several problems with this approach. It does not imitate Jesus' table ministry. Jesus invited all to the table and sat with all. If the table embodies the gospel and bears witness to the gospel, then it should reflect the universal intent of the gospel. Just as our preaching invites all to faith, so the table should invite all to eat. The table, just as the ministry of the Word, offers grace and testifies that Jesus died for all. The table is a place where sinners can not only hear but experience the gracious message of the gospel through eating with the community of faith. All are invited to eat with Jesus. The community of faith receives aliens at its table.

It is inappropriate to simply relegate this question to individual decision. The church eats and drinks as a community and we sit at the table with each other. Who sits at the table says something about the community as well as the host. The responsibility is communal, not individual. Consequently, Paul forbids the Corinthians to eat with rebellious sinners (1 Cor. 5:11). While he may mean any meal, it would surely include the Lord's meal which the assembled church ate together. The church should exclude some from the table. They judge those among themselves who are rebellious and bar the disciplined from the table.

In the same way, the church as a community invites all who would seek God through Jesus to the table. It invites the sinner, the unchurched and the weak family member to the table to hear the gospel of grace. It invites all to learn the gospel through eating and drinking. It should invite all except the disciplined who have demonstrated their disdain for the table through their rebellious lifestyle.

When the Lord's Supper is conceived as a meal at a table, then the exclusion of seekers and children (see point twelve in chapter thirteen) is incongruous with the genius of the meal. If the Lord's Supper is a meal, then it would be a counter-testimony to exclude non-Christians or children from the meal. It would deny food to the hungry, both spiritually and physically.

But should not those who eat do so in a "worthy" manner? Yes, but this is required of those who eat within the community of faith (see question 5 below). Those who are part of the community of faith must eat and drink "worthily," but those outside the community come to the table to hear the gospel, meet Jesus and experience communal love.

2. Who may serve the table? Early in the history of the church, the Eucharist became a locus of ecclesial authority. Ignatius (ca. 115), for example, counseled that only Eucharists authorized by a Bishop were legitimate (*Smyreans* 8.2). The focal point for schisms in mid-third century Carthage was the episcopal right to sanction and conduct Eucharists. Who may administer the Lord's supper? Christian traditions have generally believed that only certain ordained ministers or clerics may feed the flock through the supper. Thus, only priests in Roman Catholicism may administer the Mass and in Presbyterianism only ordained pastors may administer the Eucharist. A kind of hierarchicalism invaded the table in Christian history.

One of the primary contributions of Churches of Christ to American Christianity is the practical priesthood of all believers. While Protestants have generally advocated a universal priesthood, clerical hierarchicalism has dominated the table. The Stone-Campbell (or Restoration Movement radicalized this priesthood. Every male had access to administering and serving the table. In some sense it democratized the table, but this was a return to the primitive table. Jesus is the host of the table and everyone else is a servant-guest. The table equalizes all participants as they sit together as guests of the Living Host.

When the Lord's supper is conceived as table rather than altar, then the need for clerics and ordained priests dissipates.

An altar needs a priest, but a table only needs a host. Table guests enjoy the hospitality of host. The host of the church's table is Jesus. We are the table guests, and at this table there is no hierarchy. When the church sits together at table, they sit as servants, not clerics.

Consequently, in Churches of Christ you will see men—young and old, novice and mature, rich and poor, black and white—serve the table. All men are invited to serve. Unfortunately, yet another hierarchy invaded the table. Only males are permitted to serve the table. The very table that unites rich and poor as well as young and old is the very thing that divides male and female. Some are excluded from serving the table because of their gender. Instead of mutual servants, a hierarchical table arrangement is interposed between male and female.

But, some may ask, does not "authority" belong to males within the church? Irrespective of how we might answer that question (and I think there is a biblical principle of "male headship" rooted in creation), table is not a place of authority. It is a table of servants. When women are excluded from serving at the table, they are excluded from service, not authority. They are not permitted to imitate Jesus at the table who served his disciples, a service to which Jesus called all his disciples as a principle of love. They are denied the opportunity to serve. At any other table, women are expected to serve, but at the table of the Lord they are barred from serving.

Reimaging the supper as a table highlights the problem. If the church literally sat at a table, who passed the food would have little consequence. If the church literally sat at a table, who brought the food to the table would have little consequence except as an expression of service. The exclusion of women from serving the table is rooted in an altar-mentality where authority is linked to the altar, and it is rooted in an inappropriate formalism that turns the assembly of the saints into an institutional hierarchy rather than a domestic (family) table.

The meaning of service at the table has nothing to do with authority. On the contrary, it expresses a mutual commitment to serve each other not only at the table but beyond the table. When we serve each other at the table, we commit to serve each other in every other dimension of our life together. Ironically women are the more obvious servants Monday through Saturday, but on Sunday they are denied the opportunity to serve the table which promotes the service they provide throughout the rest of the week.

3. What is the relationship of Word and table? One formerly unchurched person recently told me about his first experience with the Lord's supper. He thought it was a snack. So he grabbed a whole piece of bread and casually ate it, and then drank several cups of the grape juice while holding the tray (much to the shock and consternation of the server) all the while thinking how minimal the refreshment was. He was totally alien not only to the form of the supper but to its meaning as well.

The form of the supper is overlaid with tradition. Whether we are sitting down, standing, going in procession to the front, drinking out of one cup or many, breaking off pieces or having them broken for us, whether it is a silent mediation (individual prayer) or celebrative communion (congregational singing), these are all matters of tradition. These forms, no matter which forms, are confusing to the alien in our midst. The confusion around the forms should be minimized as much as possible through explanations, orders of worship, individual greeting and sharing, but some confusion will always remain for the alien. Forms are formed by a long history of traditions, religious culture and shared experiences. It is natural for the unchurched to feel alien even when we are sensitive to their plight.

What I am more concerned about is that an unchurched person who visits some assemblies would have no idea of what is going on during the communion—not merely in terms of its form (some confusion will always remain until the shared experience forms them), but in terms of its theological significance. That an unchurched person could misinterpret the communion bread and juice for a snack says more about the divorce of the supper from the preached Word than it does about the naiveté of the unchurched. In fact, such a misunderstanding is a symptom of a deeper problem about how we approach worship itself.

When the supper is abstracted as an independent act of worship (one of the five as a checklist), it loses its connectedness with the Word and the worship event. I am an advocate of the Reformed tradition where the supper and the Word are bound together not only theologically but in practice. The supper is a concrete proclamation of the Word, but it is exactly its concrete character (bread and wine) which must be explained and applied. The supper needs to be joined with a preached Word from God so that not only the alien will appreciate its significance, but that the church will be reminded and will remember the work of God in Jesus Christ for them. The gospel should be proclaimed when the supper is served.

The Lord's supper is problematic for those who wish to conform the assembly to evangelistic designs or connect with the unchurched. It is a supper for the community and until the alien shares the communal experience of redemption the supper will remain alien. The church should not adjust the supper to the alien (such as remove it from the Sunday service as in Willow Creek traditions, or rush its observance), but proclaim the gospel through the supper and Word so that the alien learns the traditions of faith and redemption.

We cannot totally alleviate the discomfort of the alien. Nor do I think it is our task to do so, though we should be sensitive and love the alien as ourselves (Lev. 19:33-34). But the nature of communion is that it is communal—it is the shared experience of the redemptive presence of God in Christ. Aliens will always be distanced from communal remembrance as aliens. As they become part of the community, they will learn the forms and grow in the experience of the supper's meaning (note the example of Israel, Num. 9:14; 15:14-16). But they can only do so as members of the community—not as aliens. That, of course, is the goal of God—to usher aliens into the community of God where they are no longer aliens and strangers.[2]

4. *What does it mean to eat and drink "worthily"?* The church has variously interpreted the term "worthily." A primary misunderstanding has been to read the term as an adjective rather than an adverb. Some believe they must be "worthy" to approach the supper, that is, they must have lived a pure life before coming to the supper. Indeed, some church traditions have emphasized the need for extensive introspective examination or ecclesial examination (e.g., examination by a Pastor) before coming to the table. Roman Catholicism, for example, often required confession and penance before admittance to Mass. Consequently, many refuse to eat the supper because they feel "unworthy" due to their weaknesses.

But the word Paul uses in 1 Corinthians 11:29 is "unworthily" or "in an unworthy manner." The adverb describes the way in which a person eats and not the status of the person who is eating. Everyone is unworthy to approach the table. No one deserves to sit at the king's table. Everyone should approach the table with humility and gratitude, and never out of a sense of worthiness. We are not worthy. Luther's words are particularly helpful in this connection:

> But suppose you say, "What if I feel that I am unfit?" Answer: This also is my temptation, especially inherited from the old order under the pope when we tortured ourselves to become so perfectly pure that God might not find the least blemish in us. Because of this we became so timid that everyone was thrown into consternation, saying, "Alas, I am not worthy!" Then nature

and reason begin to contrast our unworthiness with this great and precious blessing, and it appears like a dark lantern in contrast to the bright sun, or as dung in contrast to jewels. Because nature and reason see this, such people refuse to go to the sacrament and wait until they become prepared, until one week passes into another and one half year into yet another. If you choose to fix your eye on how good and pure your are, to work toward the time when nothing will prick your conscience you will never go…He who earnestly desires grace and consolation should compel himself to go and allow no one to deter him, saying, "I would really like to be worthy, but I come not on account of any worthiness of mine, but on account of they Word, because thou hast commanded it and I want to be thy disciple, no matter how insignificant my worthiness"…If you are heavy-laden and feel your weakness, go joyfully to the sacrament and receive refreshment, comfort and strength.[3]

But we should eat and drink "worthily." The specific context in 1 Corinthians 11 is the divisive character of the assembly. The rich are eating without the poor. The assembly is divided by socio-economic factors. The Corinthians ate "unworthily" when they ate divisively. Paul does not suggest some kind of private introspection as a resolution to this problem. On the contrary, eating "worthily" is a communal concern. The church eats and drinks "worthily" when it eats and drinks as one body.

Unfortunately, some think "unworthily" refers to the private thoughts of the individual. Believers eat and drink "unworthily" when they do not sufficiently concentrate on the death of Christ, or they do not "discern" the body of Christ in the bread, or they do not meditate in silence, or they let their mind wander during the passing of the elements, or they do not reflect on their sins and ask God's forgiveness. In other words, "unworthily" becomes a bottomless pit into which we can throw anything that we think is inappropriate during the Lord's supper. We define "unworthily," then, by our preconceived ideas of what we think the supper is. This move means we must first have a good theological understanding of the supper before we decide how "unworthily" might be applied in our contemporary setting. Thus, if we think the supper is a silent, private, meditative act of piety, then we would eat "unworthily" if we acted in a way that violated that piety, even though that is not what the supper is.

Contextually, however, the emphasis of "unworthily" is communal. It is to eat the supper in a way that denies the gospel which the table proclaims. To eat "unworthily" is to eat in a way that undermines the gospel. In Corinth, they denied the gospel through their economic divisiveness. They also denied the gospel by sitting at two tables—the table of demons and the table of the Lord (1 Cor. 10:14-22). Though they ate at the table of the Lord, they denied the gospel through their immorality and idolatry.

"Unworthily," then, is not a matter of private psyche at the moment we bite down on the bread. The consequence of that perspective is that we oppress ourselves with interminable questions ("Am I thinking about the death of Christ?" "Am I too distracted?" "Did I pray?" "Should I read a scripture?" "Did I drink damnation to myself because I had to pay attention to my children rather than the bread?"). Rather, it is about the manner of eating in relation to the community and our lifestyle. Do we eat with a double mind or do we eat in commitment to the Lordship of Jesus as his disciples? Do we eat with prejudice and bias against another group within the church (racial, gender or socio-economic)? Do we eat knowing that we will pursue our own interests on Monday through Saturday? Do we eat on Sunday knowing we will deny the gospel through our lifestyle on Monday by cheating in our business, committing adultery or denying justice to minorities?

Fundamentally, then, to eat "worthily" is similar to living "worthily" (Phil. 1:27). When we live, we must live with gospel values as disciples of Jesus. When we eat, we must eat in a way that embodies gospel values as disciples of Jesus. The table must reflect the gospel; it must embody the character of its host. When we sit at the table in a way that denies the gospel, we eat "unworthily."

5. How often should the church eat and drink? The church has eaten the supper with varying frequency. Acts 2:46 testifies to a daily observance, but the church apparently settled into a weekly observance (Acts 20:7) which is the consistent witness of the second century church (*Didache*, Justin Martyr, Tertullian). Yet, even during the second century, the supper was eaten on Easter (even when it did not fall on a Sunday) and at special occasions (e.g., the anniversaries of martyrdoms, at baptisms, etc.). The third century exhibits clear evidence of daily observances (Cyprian).

Part of the "Constantinian shift," however, may be a less frequent participation in the supper. Though the church offered daily occasions for the Eucharist, participation declined partly because the pagan influx into the legal religion regarded the supper as too meager for a meal. Participation had so declined by the sixth century that the Council of Agatha (Canon 18; 506 A.D.) decreed that "none should be esteemed good Christians who did not communicate at least three times a year, at Christmas, Easter and Pentecost." The fourth Latern Council (1215 A.D.) lowered this requirement to once a year at Easter.

The Reformation at times was disturbed by the too frequent observance of the supper ("daily" tended to trivialize its meaning and signal too much superstitious dependence upon the Eucharist), but was also disturbed by the lack of piety among believers who did not eat the supper more than once or twice a year. Calvin, for example, believed that the table should "be spread at least once a week for the assembly of Christians."[4]

Lutherans and Anglicans as well as the early Methodists (Wesley) have promoted weekly observance, but Presbyterians, Baptists and later Methodists have followed monthly or quarterly cycles. British dissenter groups in the eighteenth and nineteenth century (including the Brethren) renewed the call for a weekly table, and Alexander Campbell followed their lead. Weekly observance has many advocates within the contemporary worship renewal movement.

Given this diversity within Christian history, it is little wonder that the arguments pro and con are many. Some claim weekly observance is mandatory while others think the Passover typology means that it should be an annual feast. Some think frequent observance devalues its meaning while others believe its meaning is best valued by frequent (even daily) observance.

I think the key is not necessarily what the early church did, but what the theological meaning of the Supper is. Its theology, rather than history, should shape practice and frequency. The Lord's supper is a table that embodies the gospel and testifies to the hope of the resurrection as it celebrates the resurrection of Jesus and anticipates the Messianic banquet. As a table in which the church shares a meal it is difficult to claim that to eat too often devalues its meaning. If the meal proclaims the gospel, its frequency would not undermine its meaning any more than weekly sermons might undermine it? If the supper is fundamentally a celebration of the resurrection hope as we eat in the presence of the Living Christ, a weekly eating on the day of the resurrection is imminently appropriate. If we gather each week to celebrate the resurrection in our assemblies, it seems we should come weekly to the table that is designed to celebrate that resurrection.

Theologically, and consistent with the historic practice of the church in Acts and throughout the centuries, the church should eat together at least once a week on the first day of the week in celebration of our resurrection hope. There are no theological reasons for doing otherwise. The resistance to weekly communion is due more to the way in which we presently observe the supper (private silence) than theological concerns. The resistance to weekly communion is pragmatic rather than theological.

6. *Does the Supper have a social and/or economic function?* The question seems quite odd in the contemporary church since the church presently emphasizes individual piety and private meditation. The social dimension is largely missing. The question's oddity is further highlighted by the reference to the supper's potential "economic" function. This seems quite strange since the contemporary supper is a minuscule piece of bread and a sip of juice. In its present form, the supper has no social or economic function. But should it?

Paul emphasizes the communal dimension of the supper. The church must eat as the one body of Christ. But this oneness has social implications. It transcends all cultural distinctions—it unites rich and poor, Jew and Gentile and male and female (cf. 1 Cor. 12:13). Whereas the table was the primary locus of social distinctions, the church united what culture divided. Greco-Roman culture divided society into different tables. The rich eat with the rich, the poor with the poor and the slaves with the slaves. The two worlds did not mix at the table. The clash between the Jewish and Gentile worlds was most acute at the table—what to eat and with whom to eat. Yet, the Lord's table is the one place in the fallen world where all ethnicities, genders and socio-economic stratas are redeemed. Christians eat together no matter what their social, economic or racial status in the culture.

The contemporary church needs to stress this social dimension. Bosnians and Serbians can sit at table together in a Croatian church. American Indo-Europeans and Palestinian Arabs can eat together in the church. The inner city poor and the suburban rich can eat together at the table of the Lord. African-Americans can eat with their White siblings as the gathered church of God. The church bears witness to the social dimensions of the gospel when it intentionally, deliberately and publicly testifies to the unity of the body through eating together.

When we reconceive the supper as a table, its social significance receives emphasis. The altar-mentality is conducive to individualism. People can go one by one to the altar and receive the benefit of the altar without social interaction with anyone else. However, a table has inherent social dimensions. Just as when a Jew sat at table with a Gentile, so also when a White sits at a table with an African-American sibling, the gospel is embodied in a social context. The table is a social event.

The table as an economic event, however, is certainly not obvious to contemporary believers. But in the early church, including the Agape feasts of the second and third centuries, the economic function was a primary consideration. The *koinonia* of the community in Acts 2 was, at least in part, holding things in common (*koina*), including the sharing of food. The generosity of the church was exhibited through breaking bread with each other (Acts 2:46). In Corinth Paul expected the supper to feed the hungry (1 Cor. 11:21-22). As a table, it fed the hungry and shared with the poor.

Too often the church has "spiritualized" the Lord's supper to the extent that it has no social or economic function. It is yet another compartmentalization of Christianity. Just as Christianity itself has been privatized in our culture, so the Lord's supper has been privatized. The contemporary church has given the supper a mere "spiritual" function. We tend to think of social and economic functions as "secular" or outside the mission of the church. But this misses the point of a table where food is shared and social barriers are torn down. As long as the altar mentality remains, the social and economic functions of the supper will remain hidden. But if the church returns to the table, then the social and economic functions of the supper will experience a revival.

7. May the church use leavened bread and fermented juice (wine)? Christians in the second, fifth or eight centuries would have found this question quite strange. Leavened bread was the dominant bread in the Western church till the 10th century, and is still used in the Eastern church (Greek Orthodox, etc.). Further, wine was the only sanctioned drink in both the Eastern and Western churches. This question, then, is a modern question. It would not have occurred to people in previous centuries.

The New Testament is rather imprecise when it comes to bread and drink. When it speaks of the bread of the supper, it only uses the general word for bread (*artos*) and does not specify "unleavened." When it speaks of the drink, it only uses the generic phrase "fruit of the vine" rather than any other specific term (such as "wine"). The New Testament lacks specification. The major theological reason for advocating unleavened bread and unfermented juice is the connection between the Lord's supper and the Passover. Since the Last Supper was a Passover, the model Jesus gave his disciples was unleavened bread. In addition, some argue that since "yeast" is forbidden at the Passover, even the drink was without yeast, that is, it was unfermented.

However, this places too much emphasis on the occasion of the Last Supper. (It also ignores the fact that the Passover did use fermented drink [wine] in the first century even though the Old Testament nowhere specifies the use of any drink during the Passover.) Certainly the Lord's supper fulfills the Passover, but is the Passover the only Old Testament theological background for the Lord's supper? Paul reflects on the meaning of sacrificial meals in 1 Corinthians 10:18, which is of wider significance than just the Passover. These meals did not use unleavened bread, except for the Passover. The theological typology which informs the Lord's supper is broader than simply the Passover, and these other meals certainly included leavened bread and fermented juice.

Once again, a recognition of the meal character of the Lord's supper helps reshape the question. If the Lord's supper is fundamentally a meal, it is the sharing of food which includes more than bread and drink. As a daily meal in the Jerusalem church, it would not have been limited to leavened bread (especially in the aftermath of the harvest festival—Pentecost). The daily bread would have been the bread of daily meals. The daily drink would have been the drink of daily meals.

Conclusion

There are many more questions than these seven. There are too many to address in a small book such as this. Hopefully, however, I have redirected the questions with a theological method that will help answer other questions. In addressing contemporary questions, the church should remember that the supper is a table (not an altar), that theology must shape its form, frequency and substance, and that its practice must embody gospel values.

Questions for Discussion

1. What is the practical significance of each of the questions discussed in this chapter?

2. Evaluate how thinking about the Lord's supper as a table rather than altar affects the answer to each of the questions.

3. Which response to the questions in this chapter was the most surprising? Why? Evaluate the argument presented for the answer given.

13 / REVISIONING THE LORD'S SUPPER

The previous survey of biblical texts, history, theological meaning and ecclesial practice may seem overwhelming as various "revisioning" suggestions were made as we encountered different factors in thinking about the Lord's supper. Consequently, in conclusion this chapter summarizes the previous chapters by focusing attention on the ways in which the church should, in my opinion, revision the supper.

Twelve Points

1. The church should revision the supper as a table rather than an altar. The Lord's supper is never described as an "altar" in Scripture. Instead, Paul explicitly dubs it "the Lord's table" (1 Cor. 10:21). Indeed, the table/altar distinction is rooted in the Hebrew sacrificial ritual. The blood is shed and poured at the altar, but the animal is eaten at the table. The cross is the Christian altar, but the Lord's supper is its table. The two are connected as those who eat at the table participate in the benefits of the altar, but the two are distinct.

The altar is a place where the guilty bring their sins for atonement, but the table is where the forgiven experience communion with God. The altar is a place of death and sorrow, but the table is a place of hope (life) and joy. The believer seeks reconciliation at the altar, but experiences reconciliation at the table. The altar may be a place for solemnity and silence, but the table is an occasion for celebration and interactive communion.

The Lord's supper is a meal eaten at a table. It is not a sacrifice offered at an altar. Understanding this fundamental difference will reshape the practice of the supper in the contemporary church.

2. The church should revision the supper as a meal rather than simply bread and wine. When the church broke bread in Acts, they ate food (Acts 2:46; 20:11). When Paul rebukes the Corinthian church he reminds them that they should have gathered to eat the Lord's supper rather than their own (1 Cor. 11:20). The Greek word "supper" refers to a meal; it was the evening meal of the Greco-Roman world. It is not the Lord's "snack," but the Lord's supper. The Passover meal (supper) is fulfilled in the Lord's meal (supper).

Bread and wine are special elements as they are singled out by the Lord's words at the Last Supper. But they are part of the meal itself as Jesus ate with his disciples. The bread and wine bring us into communion with the body and blood of Christ but they participate in the meal as a whole which fulfills the Passover in the kingdom of God (Lk. 22:16-18). The bread of "this is my body" is the bread of the meal and the wine of "this is my blood" is the wine of the meal. To separate the bread and wine from the meal is to remove them from their function in the meal and to miss the "table" dimension of the Lord's supper.

If the Lord's supper is a table, then it is also a meal. Would we call something "table" if it were only bread and drink? The table in the ancient world was where people ate the sacrificial meat in conjunction with bread and drink (just as in the fellowship offerings of the Old Testament). The Lord's table would be no different. At the Lord's table, we eat a meal.

3. The church should revision the supper as an experience of spiritual communion with the Triune God. A major dimension of the free church tradition (arising out of the Anabaptists of the sixteenth century) is the symbolic understanding of the Lord's supper. However, the supper is more than a mere symbol. It is a genuine communion with God through Jesus Christ in the Spirit. God is present at the table.

But this presence is not so much in the bread and wine as much as it is the presence of Jesus at the table. Jesus is the host of the table as he sits as the Living One at the table with us. The communion of the table is the communion of fellow participants as Jesus eats and drinks with us. Through Jesus, we also commune with God and the presence of Jesus is mediated by the Spirit of God. At the table, then, is the personal presence of Jesus through the Holy Spirit. As we worship in the Spirit, we encounter the living Christ at the table by whom we encounter God himself. The table, then, not only symbolizes but actualizes divine presence in our midst because Jesus sits at table with us.

Too often the symbolic interpretation of the supper has left the impression that the table is androcentric, that is, it is focused on what humans do at the table (we eat, we drink, we remember, we pledge). While nothing should discount the role of human participation in the supper, the focus should be on the divine act. The supper is theocentric, that is, God is doing something in the supper. God communes. God reconciles. God is present. God acts in the supper to share life with his people.

4. The church should revision the supper as an experience of interactive communion with the people of God. The table is a communal experience. It is not a private, individualistic moment. On the contrary, the sacrificial table in the Old Testament was shared with family and community. If the table is a meal, then it is interactive because meals are interactive. Tables are filled with conversation. The table is a place for fellowship where people share their lives with each other.

Unfortunately, the church practices the supper in private silence. But this is unlike any table that I have experienced. Indeed, the only table where private silence is valued is the Lord's table as it is currently practiced in the church. Yet, this undermines the very nature of table and the function of communal fellowship that table should serve. A "private table" is a meal for one, but the Lord's meal is where we "discern" the church and enjoy the fellowship of fellow believers.

Believers should experience the table as a time for sharing, prayer and conversation about what God has done for us. It is shared thanksgiving, shared commitment and shared life. The table should not be silent. Rather, it should call us to engage each other—to bear witness, to give thanks, to rehearse God's mighty acts, to pray. It is a time to experience community in contrast to withdrawing into the private recesses of the mind.

5. The church should revision the supper as an experience of grace. Too often the church has experienced the supper as a burden as some have created the expectation of near perfection in order to sit at the table. The emphasis on introspection in the history of the church has created a climate of guilt which hinders many from coming to the table. Consequently, many come to the table in fear of judgment rather than expecting grace. Therefore, they stay away from the table or fail to eat/drink because they consider themselves unworthy.

The invitation to the table, however, is an invitation to grace. God invites us to sit at table with him, not because we are worthy, but because he is gracious, forgiving and reconciling. The table testifies to the grace of the gospel. It proclaims the death of Christ as good news.

When we feel burdened with guilt and sin, we should not run from the table, but to the table. God offers his reconciling, gracious presence at the table. If we eat in faith, God receives us and gives us his presence. At the table, we can find forgiveness through faith as we experience again peace. When we eat and drink in faith, we are assured that we commune with the body and blood of Christ which is our forgiveness. As surely as we eat the bread and drink the cup, so we know that we are Christ's and his body/blood have freed us from our sins.

6. *The church should revision the supper as an experience of hope and joy.* The altar mentality is most clearly seen in the dominant mood of the contemporary practice of the supper—sorrow. The church has focused the supper on the death of Christ so that we eat and drink in sadness as we remember our sins and Christ's pain. The church has evoked images of blood and gore at the supper, and participants feel guilty if they do not concentrate on the cross and Christ's death as they eat and drink.

But no example of the supper in Scripture is so characterized. On the contrary, they are all filled with joy, hope and thanksgiving. The Old Testament sacrificial meals were joyous festivals. Even at the Last Supper, the anticipation of Christ's work to forgive sin, the fulfillment of the Passover in the coming kingdom and thanksgiving for the body and blood shape it into one of joy and hope. The Passover was supposed to be a time of joy and thanksgiving as the people anticipated the appearance of the Messiah. Even though Jesus speaks about sacrificing his body and blood on the altar, he expects to eat again with his disciples at the table in the coming kingdom. He offers a message of hope.

The practice of the supper in Luke 24, Acts 2 and Acts 20 is filled with joy. It is focused on the resurrection of Jesus rather than the death of Christ. It is the experience of the living Christ, not a dead one. It is true that the supper proclaims the death of Christ (1 Cor. 11:26), but the death of Christ is good news for those at the table. We give thanks for the reconciling work of Christ that enables the table experience of peace, hope and joy.

7. *The church should revision the supper as a socio-ethical witness through shared food.* As a table and a meal, the supper bears witness to the communal character of the Christian faith.

Just as worshippers in the Old Testament shared their sacrificial meat with family and community, so Christians shared their food with their community. The Lord's supper is an example of economic ethics as early Christians shared their resources (food) with others, particularly those in need. Consequently, the meal served the poor in the Christian community. It was the community's fellowship, their *koinonia*, as they held everything in common (*koina*).

Thus, the Lord's supper bears witness to the Christian commitment to the poor and mutual service through sharing. The church, then, should invite the poor, the disenfranchised and the outsider to share food with them as a witness to the grace of God. The supper should embody the church's rejection of materialism and demonstrate the kind of love that is willing to share material resources with the needy.

8. *The church should revision the supper as ethical commitment to the Lordship of Christ.* When we accept Christ's invitation to his table and affirm our union with him, we commit ourselves to his Lordship. We cannot sit at both the table of the Lord and the table of demons (1 Cor. 10:21). We cannot come to the table with dual commitments; we cannot serve two masters. We cannot sit at the table on Sunday and then sit at the table of immorality on Monday. We cannot share the story of Christ on Sunday and then create our own story in autonomous freedom throughout the rest of the week. When we eat, we covenant to follow Christ and pledge again to be the people of God in the world. At the table every week we rededicate ourselves to God's story.

As we sit at the table of Lord in the kingdom of God, we are reminded that we are citizens of kingdom and disciples of Jesus. We commit to follow the example of Christ and to live a life worthy of the gospel (Phil. 1:27). This commitment to follow Jesus ultimately means that we take up our cross and follow his example of sacrificial living. We are obedient servants, even to the cross.

9. The church should revision the supper as the visible, concrete display of the unity of the body of Christ. When at the table, the church exhibits their "common union" in Christ. What unites them is not their socio-economic status, gender, nationality or ethnicity, but their union with Christ. They commune with each other because they already commune with Christ.

But this union must have visible expression. A "spiritual" union is inadequate if it has no concrete expression or meaning. In the church, the table is the place where this visible unity is most concretely demonstrated as the people of God eat and drink together. As one body we eat one bread and drink from one cup.

10. The church should revision the supper as a moment of inclusiveness that transcends all cultural, ethnic and gender boundaries. We sit at table with Christ and we are at the table because Christ has invited us. It is his table. Consequently, we do not choose who sits at the table; Christ does. We must receive whoever sits at the table because Christ has invited them.

The table, then, is the place where the church testifies to the world how it transcends all worldly distinctions. In the church, male and female sit at the table together. In the church, white and black sit at the table together. In the church, the rich and poor sit at the table together. The oneness of the body, with all its cultural, ethnic and gender diversity, is given visible expression when in the church people who are divided in the world sit at one table and eat from one bread.

But this inclusiveness is not simply a tolerance for others. It is an attitude of service. We sit at the table not simply as guests, but as servants. We are not only servants of Jesus, but mutual servants. At the table we commit to serve each other. As we raise the cup and drink together, we mutually pledge to "be there" for each other. As we break the bread and eat together, we mutually commit to give our lives for each other, just as Jesus gave his life for us.

11. The church should revision the supper as the participation of all except the rebellious. The Lord's supper is a table event; a meal which the community of faith shares. The community invites all to share the meal with them as a witness to the truth and meaning of the gospel. All are invited; none but the rebellious are barred.

The table, as the place of hospitality in the church of God, is where all are welcomed just as the grace of God is for all. Jesus ate with all kinds of people—the tax collector as well as the Pharisee, women as well as men, the poor as well as the rich. The table bears witness to the universal call of the gospel. Just as the gospel calls everyone to faith, so does the table. Just as grace is extended to all who will receive it, the table is available for all who will come. We do not exclude guests from singing, hearing the gospel or even giving, and neither should we exclude them from the table.

However, there is one class who are excluded from the table. The rebellious, like the incestuous son of 1 Corinthians 5, are excluded. While we do not judge the world and exclude them from the table of grace, we do judge community members. The church should not eat with rebellious family members who refuse to submit to the Lordship of Christ (1 Cor. 5:11-13).

12. The church should revision the supper as a family event, including children. The supper was originally experienced in the context of a meal. Neither guests nor children would have been excluded from that meal. It was for everyone as a witness to the grace of God, which is for everyone. The table was a function of hospitality.

Children are invited to the table because they are part of the community of faith; they belong to the kingdom. They are kingdom people. They are on the journey of faith, and the supper will shape the growth and development of that faith. The supper testifies to the faithfulness and love of God, and when children eat, they experience that faithfulness and love at the table. The table, then, is a learning event for children. They hear the story of the gospel and participate in the elements, which bear witness to the gospel. They experience the gospel through eating and drinking. This prepares their heart for discipleship, encourages the development of their faith, and assures them of God's love on their journey.

Baptism is where our children commit themselves to the way of the cross as disciples of Jesus. Baptism is partly an individual act of faith-commitment. The table is where children learn about Jesus and experience his love. The table is family time; it is a communal event. As part of the family—as persons on the journey of faith—they should sit at the table with the rest of the community. It is unwise to send children to bed without their supper, and it is potentially a hindrance to their faith to exclude them from the table in the family of God.

Exhortation

"Revisioning" is a difficult process. It is difficult because it is hard to look past our own contextual factors to see the table with the eyes of God in the light of biblical theology. It is difficult because it creates dissonance between ourselves and our immediate heritage. It is difficult because its implementation is fraught with logistic, practical, and communal problems.

Yet, we must commit ourselves to see the table with God's eyes, reject what is inconsistent with that vision (even if it runs counter to our heritage), and actualize the table in our communities in accordance with that vision. The first step is personal prayer and Bible study. The second is communal prayer and discussion. The third step is communal consensus. The fourth step is communal practice.

Since the supper intends to display the unity of the people of God, it must not become the source of dissension and division. The table should be revisioned, but it ought not divide. I do not call for forced change or heavy-handed tactics. On the contrary, I call for communal prayer, study and reflection. In that context the Lord's table can take center stage as the visible unity of Lord's people and function as *koinonia* (communion) between believers and with the Lord as host.

Conclusion

In the beginning God created life; the divine community created a community to share love. Out of love, God invited his people to eat and share his life. God provided a table; God sought *koinonia* (fellowship) with his people.

Humanity rejected the invitation. They created their own community and sat at a different table. They asserted their moral autonomy and fell into sin. As a consequence, they were excluded from the divine community and its table (the Garden).

God, however, still sought *koinonia* (fellowship) with his people. He acted to redeem. He called Abraham and created a nation. He gave Israel his presence and through the altar invited Israel to share his table. He renewed fellowship with his people and the people experienced the presence of God at table. But Israel often disgraced that table and dishonored God even while eating at the table (cf. Ps. 50).

Nevertheless, in Jesus Christ God demonstrated his unfailing love. In Jesus, God dwelt among his people and sat at table with sinners as well as saints. Jesus invited all to his table and extended God's love to everyone. At table, Jesus demonstrated God's ultimate intent to fellowship his people. But humanity killed the Son of God.

Nevertheless, God raised Jesus from the dead and poured out his Spirit upon the church. God raised up yet another table for the people of God where he would commune with his people. At table, the church communes with the risen Lord and with each other. But often the church fails to embody the gospel at that table.

Nevertheless, God will actualize the fullness of his kingdom. He will fulfill his table intentions in the coming kingdom. In the new heaven and new earth, God will set a table for his servants who are waiting for that kingdom (Lk. 12:35-38). The only question is whether the Son of Man, when he returns, will find faith on the earth (Lk. 18:8). Will he find a church sitting at table with each other, sharing their food, embodying the values of the gospel, and waiting for the Messianic banquet?

Just as the parable of the prodigal son ended, so does this book (Lk. 15:32). It ends with a question mark. Will the elder brother "celebrate and rejoice" at the table with his lost, but now found, brother? Will the church of God "celebrate and rejoice" at the table in the living presence of Christ as his cruciform disciples? Will we eat and drink in faith, hope and love as we wait for the return of the Son of Man?

Questions for Discussion

1. Which of the twelve points seem to offer the most signifiant revisioning for your congregation?

2. Which of the twelve points do you find most problematic?

3. Which of the twelve points do you find most enlightening?

4. Which of the twelve points do you think your congregation should most seriously consider as you examine your practice of the supper?

Recommended Reading

*An asterisk means that the recommended reading is especially significant as supportive of the point of this book.

Biblical and Theological Materials
*Barth, Markus. *Rediscovering the Lord's Supper: Communion with Israel, with Christ, and Among Guests.* Atlanta: John Knox, 1988.

Berquist, Jon L. *Ancient Wine, New Wineskins: The Lord's Supper in Old Testament Perspective.* St. Louis: Chalice Press, 1991.

*Cochrane, Arthur C. *Eating and Drinking with Jesus: An Ethical and Biblical Inquiry.* Philadelphia: Westminster, 1974.

Feeley-Harnik, Gillian. *The Lord's Table: The Meaning of Food in Early Judaism and Christianity.* Washington: Smithsonian Institution Press, 1994.

Jeremias, Joachim. *The Eucharistic Words of Jesus.* Translated by Norman Perrin. Philadelphia: Fortress, 1966.

Koenig, John. *The Feast of the World's Redemption: Eucharistic Origins and Christian Mission.* Harrisburg, PA: Trinity International, 2000.

Kodell, Jerome. *The Eucharist in the New Testament.* Collegeville, MN: Liturgical Press, 1988.

*LaVerdiere, Eugene. *The Breaking of the Bread: The Development of the Eucharist according to the Acts of the Apostles.* Chicago: Liturgy Training Publications, 1998.

*LaVerdiere, Eugene. *Dining in the Kingdom of God: The Origins of the Eucharist in the Gospel of Luke.* Chicago: Liturgy Training Publications, 1994.

*LaVerdiere, Eugene. *The Eucharist in the New Testament and the Early Church.* Collegeville, MN: Liturgical Press, 1996.

McElvaney, William K. *Eating and Drinking at the Welcome*

Table: The Holy Supper for All People. St. Louis: Chalice Press, 1998.

Marshall, I. Howard. *Last Supper and Lord's Supper.* Grand Rapids: Eerdmans, 1980.

Moloney, Francis J. *A Body Broken for a Broken People: Eucharist in the New Testament.* Peabody, MA: Hendrickson, 1997.

*Smith, Dennis E. and Hal E. Taussig. *Many Tables: The Eucharist in the New Testament and Liturgy Today.* Philadelphia: Trinity International, 1990.

Yoder, John Howard. *Body Politics: Five Practices of the Christian Community Before the Watching World.* Nashville: Discipleship Resources, 1992.

Historical Materials

*Gresham, Charles R. and Tom Lawson. *The Lord's Supper: Historical Writings On Its Meaning to the Body of Christ.* Joplin, MO: College Press, 1993.

Jasper, R. C. D. and G. J. Cuming, eds. *Prayers of the Eucharist: Early and Reformed.* 2nd edition. New York: Oxford University, 1980.

*McGowan, Andrew Brian. *Ascetic Eucharists: Food and Drink in Early Christian Ritual Meals.* New York: Oxford University, 1999.

O'Connor, James T. *The Hidden Manna: A Theology of the Eucharist.* San Francisco: St. Ignatius Press, 1988.

Sasse, Hermann. *This is My Body: Luther's Contention for the Real Presence in the Sacrament of the Altar.* Revised Edition. Adelaide: Lutheran Publishing House, 1977.

*Stoffer, Dale R. *The Lord's Supper: Believers Church Perspectives.* Scottsdale, PA: Herald Press, 1997.

Rempel, John D. *The Lord's Supper in Anabaptism: A Study in the Christology of Balthasar Hubmaier, Pilgram Marpeck, and Dirk Philips.* Studies in Anabaptist and Mennonite History, No. 33. Scottdale, PA: Herald Press, 1993.

Rordorf, Willy. *The Eucharist of the Early Christians*. Translated by Matthew J. O'Connell. New York: Pueblo Publishing Co., 1978.

White, James F. *The Sacraments in Protestant Practice and Faith*. Nashville: Abingdon, 1999.

Devotional, Homiletical and Practical Materials

Gondola, Alex., Jr. *Come As You Are: Sermons on the Lord's Supper*. Lima, Ohio: CSS Publishing Co., Inc., 2000.

Henry, Jim. I*n Remembrance of Me: A Manual on Observing the Lord's Supper*. Nashville: Broadman & Holman Publishers, 1998.

Kerr, Hugh Thomson. *The Christian Sacraments: A Source Book for Ministers*. Philadelphia: Westminster, 1944.

Lewis, Warren. *The Lord's Supper*. Austin, TX: R. B. Sweet., 1966.

Nichol, C. R. *The Lord's Supper, Prayers: The Institution of the Lord's Supper, the Observance of the Supper, Thanks, Prayers for All Occasions*. Clifton, TX: Nichol Publishing Co., 1957.

*Richardson, Robert. *Communings in the Sanctuary*. Introduced and edited by C. Leonard Allen. Orange, CA: New Leaf Books, 2000; reprint of 1872 ed.

*Willimon, William H. *Sunday Dinner: The Lord's Supper and the Christian Life*. Nashville: The Upper Room, 1981.

NOTES

Chapter 1

1. This material is largely derived from the third chapter of my *Yet Will I Trust Him: Understanding God in a Suffering World* (Joplin, MO: College Press, 1999).

2. For good resources on the social understanding of the Trinity, see Peter Toon, *Our Triune God: A Biblical Portrayal of the Trinity* (Wheaton: Victor Books, 1996) and Catherine Mowry LaCugna, *God For Us: The Trinity & Christian Life* (San Francisco: HarperSanFrancisco, 1991). Ted Peters, *God as Trinity: Relationality and Temporality in Divine Life* (Louisville: Westminster/John Knox Press, 1993), surveys current discussions of trinitarian theology.

3. John Piper, *Desiring God: Meditations of a Christian Hedonist* (Portland, OR: Multnomah Press, 1986).

Chapter 3

1. Walther Eichrodt, *Theology of the Old Tetament* (Philadelphia: Westminster, 1961), 1:156.

2. Ibid., 1:157-8.

3. Based on E. P. Sanders, *Judaism: Practice and Belief, 63 BCE-66 CE* (Philadelphia: Trinity International, 1992), 110-116.

4. See Dennis R. Lindsay, "Todah and Eucharist: The Celebration of the Lord's Supper as a 'Thank Offering' in the Early Church," *Restoration Quarterly* 39 (1997), 83-100.

Chapter 4

1. Markus Barth, *Resdiscovering the Lord's Supper* (Atlanta: John Knox, 1988), 71. On the importance of meals in Luke-Acts, see Jerome H. Neyrey, "Ceremonies in Luke-Acts: The Case of Meals and table Fellowship," in *The Social World of Luke-Acts*, ed. Jerome H. Neyrey (Peabody, MA: Hendrickson, 1991), 361-87, Robert Karris, *Luke: Artist and Theologian* (New York: Paulist, 1985), 47-78 and Dennis E. Smith, "Table Fellowship as a Literary Motif in the Gospel of Luke," *Journal of Biblical Literature* 106.4 (1987), 613-38.

2. John Koenig, *The Feast of the World's Redemption: Eucharistic Origins and Christian Mission* (Harrisbug, PA: Trinity Press International, 2000), 181.

3. I constructed this chart and adapted much of the material from Eugene LaVerdiere, *Dining in the Kingdom of God: The Origins of the Eucharist in the Gospel of Luke* (Chicago: Liturgy Training Publications, 1994). For those interested in a full analysis of these meals in the light of Luke's purposes, LaVerdiere's work is necessary reading.

4. Ibid., 69.

5. Ibid., 85.

6. William H. Willimon, *Sunday Dinner: The Lord's Supper and the Christian Life* (Nashville: Upper Room, 1981), 59.

7. LaVerdiere, *Dining in the Kingdom*, 171.

8. Barth, *Rediscovering*, 71.

9. Jerome Kodell, *The Eucharist in the New Testament* (Collegeville, MN: Liturgical Press, 1988), 107.

10. Barth, *Rediscovering*, 74.

11. Kodell, *Eucharist*, 110.

12. Barth, *Rediscovering*, 73

Chapter 5

1. See I. Howard Marshall, *Last Supper and Lord's Supper* (Grand Rapids: Eerdmans, 1980), 57-75.

2. Ibid., 179. For more details and a correlation with the Lord's supper, see Norman Theiss, "The Passover Feast of the New Covenant," *Interpretation* 48 (Jan 1994), 17-31. The classic discussion is Joachim Jeremias, *The Eucharistic Words of Jesus* (Philadelphia: Fortress, 1966), 15-88.

Chapter 6

1. The fullest defense of an eucharistic understanding of "break-ing bread" is Eugene LaVerdiere, *The Breaking of the Bread: The Development of the Eucharist According to Acts* (Chicago: Liturgy Training Publications, 1998).

One other "breaking bread" story is Acts 27:35. This is the most difficult text for construing "breaking bread" as meaning a religious or Christological meal. One cannot be certain about its meaning, but it is likely, given the language used, that the first Christian readers would have used the Lord's supper as a frame of reference for under-standing this meal on the ship. Paul used the meal as a means of encouragement and assurance. Eating represented hope: all would be saved, so all ate. If this is a eucharistic breaking of bread, it teach-es the church that the Supper is about hope and inclusivism, that is, that all are invited to share in the salvation of God, even pagan Roman soldiers.

There are contextual considerations for thinking that this is at least an allusion to the Christian supper, if not an actual instance of celebrating it. Nothing is ordinary about this meal, especially in the light of Luke's portrayal of Paul on this journey (Reicke, "Die Mahlzeit mit Paulus auf den Wellen des Mittelmeers, Acta 27:33-38," *Theolo-gische Zeitschrift* 4 [1948], 401-10; cf. the appearance of the angel). The eucharistic language is striking as it connects with other Lucan texts (v.35, and v.34 connects with 2:46 in the term *metalambano*). C. K. Barrett, "Paul Shipwrecked," in *Scripture: Meaning and Method*, ed. Barry P. Thompson (North Yorkshire: Hull University, 1987), 60, writes: "It seems unthinkable that Luke should have forgotten that he had written at significant points in his gospel the words that he uses here, and very improbable that the words were not used, and were not known by him to be used, by the church of which he was a member at its regular meeting for Supper."

The story also fits Luke's emphasis on Jew-Gentile table fellow-ship as the symbol of community (Philip Francis Esler, *Community and Gospel in Luke-Acts: The Social and Political Motivations of Lucan Theology* [Cambridge: Cambridge University Press, 1987]). The language surrounding the text is filled with soteriological imagery (not a soul will be lost, v.22; "do not be afraid," v.24; God's graciousness, v.24; faith in God, v.25; salvation, v.31; brought safely through, v.44/28:1; everyone was encouraged, v.36). The parallel structures of Luke and Acts: trials, imprisonment, climatic events, etc., give this meal a parallel with the Last Supper in Luke 22 (M. D. Goulder, *Type and History in Acts* [London: S.P.C.K., 1964] and C. Talbert, *Literary Patterns, Theological Themes and the Genre of Luke-Acts* [Missoula: Scholars Press, 1974]). Further, the text is the most eucharistic text in Acts. Only here does "give thanks" and "to take the bread" occur in Acts in a way that parallels Luke 22:19. For other defenses of an eucharistic understanding of Acts 27:35, see D. Richardson, "The Place of Luke in the Eucharistic Tradition," *Studia Evangelica*, TU 73 (Berlin: Akadamie-Verlag, 1959), 671-72 and J. Dupont, "The Meal at Emmaus," in *The Eucharist in the New Testament*, ed. J. Delorme, P. Benoit, and M. E. Boismard and trans. by E. M. Stewart (Baltimore: Helicon Press, 1965), 105-21.

However, since this is a highly disputed text, I have set it aside for the purposes of this chapter.

2. LaVerdiere, *Dining in the Kingdom*, 174.

3. Ibid., 174.

4. John Howard Yoder, *Body Politics: Five Practices of the Christian Community Before the Watching World* (Nashville: Discipleship Resources, 1992), 20.

5. Ibid., 21.

6. Max M. B. Turner, "The Sabbath, Sunday, and the Law in Luke/Acts," in *From Sabbath to Lord's Day: A Biblical, Historical and Theological Investigation*, ed. D. A. Carson (Grand Rapids: Zondervan, 1982), 128-30.

7. For an extended defense of the theological significance of the first day of the week, see D.A. Carson, ed., *From Sabbath to Lord's Day*.

8. Barth, *Rediscovering*, 74.

Chapter 7

1. A. C. Thiselton, "Realized Eschatology at Corinth," *New Testament Studies* 24 (1977/78), 510-26. The commentary by Gordon

D. Fee, *The First Epistle to the Corinthians*, NICNT (Grand Rapids: Eerdmans, 1987), 10-15, follows this perspective.

2. The commentary by Richard E. Oster, *1 Corinthians* (Joplin, MO: College Press, 1995), 23-25, follows this perspective.

3. Oster, *1 Corithians*, 24.

4. Francis J. Moloney, *A Body Broken for a Broken People: Eucharist in the New Testament* (Peabody, MA: Hendrickson, 1997), 161.

5. Fee, *Epistle to the Corinthians*, 467.

Chapter 8

1. Dennis E. Smith and Hal E. Taussig, *Many Tables: The Eucharist in the New Testament and Liturgy Today* (Philadelphia: Trinity International, 1990), 25.

2. Aristophanes, *Acharnenses*, 1085-1149; Xenophon, *Memorabilia*, 3.14.1; Aelius Aristides, *Sarapis*, 54.20-28; Lucian, *Lexiphanes*, 6,9,13; cf. Peter Lampe, "The Eucharist: Identifying with Christ on the Cross," *Interpretation* 48 (Jan 1994), 37-41.

3. Rick Oster, "Going to Worship in Ancient Corinth," *Leaven* 6 (Winter 1998), 16-17.

4. One Latin inscription from Pompeii stated, "Be sociable and put aside, if you can, annoying quarrels. If you can't, go back to your own home" (Oster, *1 Corinthians*, 277).

Chapter 9

1. Quotations from the Didache are from *The Apostolic Fathers*, edited and translated by J. B. Lightfoot and J. R. Harmer; 2nd ed., edited and revised by Michael W. Holmes (Grand Rapids: Baker, 1992), 259-63.

2. Eugene LaVerdiere, *The Eucharist in the New Testament and the Early Church* (Collegevill, MN: Liturgical Press, 1996), 140.

3. Cf. Raymond Johanny, "Ignatius of Antioch," in *The Eucharist of the Early Christians*, ed. by Willy Rordorf (New York: Pueblo Publishing Co., 1978), 48-70.

4. *Apostolic Fathers*, 161.

5. Ibid., 179.

6. Andrew McGowan, "Water in the Desert: Wine, Eucharist and

Sacrifice in Tertullian and Cyprian," [paper presented at the 1998 annual meeting of the American Academy of Religion, available at http://divinity.library.vanderbilt.edu/burns/chroma/eucharist/euchM cGowan.html], argues that Cyprian is the main advocate of sacrificial language while it is absent in Tertullian.

7. John Howard Yoder, "The Constantianian Sources of Western Social Ethics," in *The Priestly Kingdom: Social Ethics as Gospel* (Notre Dame, IN: University of Notre Dame Press, 1984), 135ff.

8. Jeff Bach, "The Agape in the Brethren Tradition," in *The Lord's Supper: Believer's Church Perspectives,* ed. by Dale R. Stoffer (Scottdale, PA: Herald Press), 161-8.

9. Leigh Eric Schmidt, *Holy Fairs: Scottish Communion and American Revivals in the Early Modern Period* (Princeton: Princeton University, 1989).

10. Cited by Alexander Campbell, "Attempt at the Restoration of Ancient Order," *Christian Baptist* 5 (November 5, 1827), 389-90 [Burnet edition] and 5 (February 4, 1828), 414-15 [Burnet edition].

11. Lynn A. McMillon, "Discovery of the Earliest Extant Scottish Restoration Congregation," *Restoration Quarterly* 30 (1988), 43-51.

12. Alexander Campbell, "Breaking the Loaf," in *The Christian System* (Nashville: Gospel Advocate, 1970, reprint of 1839 edition), 265.

13. Ibid., 269.

14. Campbell, "Meeting-Houses," *Millennial Harbinger* 5 (January 1834), 8.

15. Campbell, "Breaking the Loaf," 291.

16. Campbell, "A Restoration of the Ancient Order of Things— No. XV. Love Feasts." *Christian Baptist* 4 (November 1826): 282-284 (Burnet edition).

17. Moses Lard, "My Church," *Lard's Quarterly* 1 (1864), 150.

18. Marlin Jeschke, "Making the Lord's Supper Meaningful," in *The Lord's Supper: Believers Church Perspectives,* ed. by Dale R. Stoffer (Scottdale, PA: Herald Press, 1997), 151-2.

Chapter 10

1. This material originally appeared as "The Lord's Table: A Covenant Meal," *Leaven* 3.3 (1995), 4-7.

2. Yoder, *Body Politics*, 20.

Chapter 11

1. For some help with this text, see chapter six in this book and my article at http://johnmarkhicks.faithsite.com/content.asp?CID= 6792.

Chapter 12

1. John Mark Hicks, "Alexander Campbell on Christians Among the Sects," in *Baptism and the Remission of Sins*, ed. David Fletcher (Joplin, MO: College Press, 1990), 171-202, available at http://johnmarkhicks.faithsite.com/content.asp? CID=10070.

2 This answer to the question was first published as "Teach the Gospel as Part of the Lord's Supper," *Christian Chronicle* 53.6 (June 1996), 20, available at http://johnmarkhicks.faithsite.com/content .asp?CID=6493.

3. Martin Luther, "Large Catechism," in *The Book of Concord: The Confessions of the Evangelical Lutheran Church*, trans. and ed. by Theodore G. Tappert (Philadelphia: Fortress Press, 1959), 471.

4. John Calvin, *Institutes of the Christian Religion* in Library of Christian Classics, ed. John T. McNeill and trans.. Ford Lewis Battles (Philadelphia: Westminster, 1960), IV.17.46.

Also Available

THE GREAT RESCUE
The Story of God's Amazing Grace

Edward William Fudge

'The Great Rescue is at once a gripping novel and a compelling theology text. It unfolds the sweeping panorama of God's redemptive work. The resulting picture is truly a masterpiece of grace."
    —James Sweeney, Provost
        Western Seminary, Portland, OR

150 pages, paper   9.95

CEASEFIRE
Ending Worship Wars through Sound Theology and Plain Common Sense

Perry C. Cotham

An engaging introduction to Christian worship, with an eye to the current "worship wars" among churches. Twelve fresh, remarkably balanced, and challenging chapters, along with extensive questions for disussion.

266 pages, paper   14.95

Available through your Christian bookstore
Or call toll free 1-877-634-6004

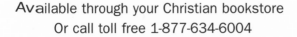

New Leaf Books